THE LAYMAN'S GUIDE
TO **M**AKING
SENSE OF
STATISTICS

THE LAYMAN'S GUIDE
TO **M**AKING **S**ENSE OF **S**TATISTICS

JOHN L. CAMPBELL

Kravitz & Sons
INNOVATORS IN PUBLISHING, MARKETING AND ADVERTISING

The excerpt from Distribution-Free Statistical Tests (1968) by James V. Bradley is reprinted herein by permission of Simon & Schuster.

Kravitz and Sons LLC
1301 Farmville Blvd, Suite 104
Greenville, NC 27834

Published by Kravitz and Sons LLC.

ISBN: 979-8-89639-251-4 (sc)
ISBN: 979-8-89639-273-6 (hb)
ISBN: 979-8-89639-252-1 (e)

Library of Congress Control Number: 2025907867

In the furtherance of understanding

PREFACE

Nearly all books about statistics are textbooks for college students preparing to work in a field of endeavor requiring a professional's understanding of statistical concepts and techniques. Often these texts double as reference books consulted by individuals already in that field. Fields - professions - heavily into statistics include economics, business, psychology, sociology, education, public health, and medicine. The effects on society of applying to it the results of the statistical analyses performed daily in such fields run the gamut from shaping people's attitudes and determining the products and services they receive to molding public policy and evaluating ways of doing things. It thus seems everybody who is not one of these professionals ought to have a practical knowledge about statistics and hence be statistically literate.

The title of this book indicates the book is for people ignorant of statistics. However, people fairly knowledgeable of statistics may find insights in it they can profitably apply. The book is intended to instill statistical literacy. Its concern with literacy makes it akin to my book intended to instill scientific literacy (Campbell, 2025). Probably most readers of this preface don't want to learn how to perform calculations with statistics and are only after the gist of statistics. This is not surprising. After all, people today needing these calculations are spared the drudgery which typically faced people needing them fifty years ago. For today there are affordable personal computers that, when equipped with statistical software packages, process in minutes the data inputted into them, data that fifty years ago took hours to process using less sophisticated equipment. Today, too, there are inexpensive handheld calculators which, while not as versatile as PCs, beat how statistical calculations were once done.

I recommend that you first skim this book, next read it thoroughly, and finally read it thoroughly again a month or two later. That way you will benefit from the pedagogical principle of distributed practice that facilitates the learning of tough topics. Should you later on wish to know how to perform statistical calculations you will need to consult a textbook, since you won't find in this book any formulae, equations, or exercises which pertain to calculating the statistics it discusses. Despite the book being introductory, it covers some material in greater detail than many introductory statistics texts do. Hence do not be deceived by its lack of formulae, equations, and exercises. The reason behind the greater detail is that the book was written with two audiences in mind.

Some readers *want to learn statistics* to know better the things heard or read which cite statistical information. Others *need to learn statistics* because knowing statistics is necessary or desirable in their line of work. Examples of readers of the second kind are individuals who routinely review statistical reports submitted to them and make important decisions or recommendations based on what (they understand) these reports are to say. While writing this book I have tried to heed the advice of Albert Waugh (1943, p vii): "One of the most difficult problems in writing any elementary textbook is to keep it truly elementary, to write for beginning students rather than for one's colleagues".

John L. Campbell
Roseburg, Or 97470

May 2025

Contents

CHAPTER 1

SOME HISTORICAL PERSPECTIVE

Let us begin by clarifying what's meant by statistics. Statistics has three meanings. First, it means observations of something by someone (i.e., what a person sees, hears, touches, smells, etc.). Such observations are popularly called facts and are subdivided into data and information*. They are referred to as data if either simple or relatively unorganized and as information if either complex or relatively organized. Hence statistics means observations, facts, data, or information about something, something observable and thus able to be observed (seen, heard, felt, smelled, etc.). Statistics, so construed, takes the form of numbers, words, or mixtures of both. This first meaning of statistics arose about 1800 as the name for observations of characteristics of populations of people (note that populations of things other than people exist too). Many characteristics of human populations are of a socioeconomic (social or economic) nature. Vital statistics and labor statistics are observations that are ordinarily data and which address two human population characteristics, life and livelihood.

Second, statistics means the profession that supplies other professions with concepts and techniques they need for processing data. Data processing is the transforming of less useful data into more useful information. Construed as a profession, statistics took shape around 1835 and in about 1890 became a branch of mathematics. Third, since around 1950 statistics has meant the information in samples generated from data from populations, a statistic being a type of information about samples or, in other words, a type of sample information. Statistics, viewed as sample information, are usually mixtures of numbers and words. Now the context within which the word statistics occurs will suggest which of its three meanings is intended.

Therefore 'statistics' was coined around 1800 as the name for observations pertaining to human populations. Then, in about 1835, statistics came to also signify the profession furnishing other professions with the conceptual and technical tools they need to process their data and thereby make data into information. Finally, around 1950, statistics came to additionally mean sample information. It's important to understand that the advent of the word statistics did not signal the birth of collecting and processing data on human population characteristics. Those activities had by 1800 been going on a long time. Nevertheless, its advent coincided with a mounting interest in socioeconomic data by capitalists excited about the socioeconomic implications of the rapidly unfolding Industrial Revolution and by social philosophers hoping to implement the dreams set forth in the recent Age of Enlightenment/ Age of Reason (circa 1690-1790).

In what follows we sketch the history, up to approximately 1900, of collecting and processing data on human populations. To simplify matters, we will from here onward refer to said data as data, not statistics, and thus limit our use of the word statistics to its second meaning (the profession statistics) and third meaning (sample information).

Curiosity and a need to know the characteristics of one's own population and of the populations of one's neighbors grow as their populations grow. And as these populations grow from dozens to hundreds to thousands to millions of people — from villages to towns to cities to nations — the observations (chiefly data) behind this knowledge tend to grow steadily in quality from the few and unplanned observations yielding what is known as anecdotal knowledge to the many and planned observations giving rise to systematic knowledge. It is the many planned observations making up a systematic knowledge about populations that we will concentrate on. Consequently, our journey into the past looks largely at populations which, in their day, were nations.

Need more than curiosity has inspired most studies designed to get population data. Hence a definitely practical air has mostly surrounded these studies. This should come as no surprise. It takes substantial time and effort to locate all, even most, inhabitants of a population, observe them, and record what is observed (i.e., record the observations made, typically seen as data collected). What needs could justify such vast outlays of time and energy? Many relate to a population's socioeconomic characteristics. Now by knowing certain socioeconomic characteristics the ruler of a nation is able to rule more effectively. For instance, knowing the number of able-bodied men a nation has lets its ruler know how large an army his nation can have for defending itself, or for attacking a neighbor. And knowing their country has experienced over the last few years rising surpluses in its yearly harvesting of wheat and that a neighboring country's annual wheat harvest during those years usually fell short of meeting its needs, wheat farmers of the first country know they have a potential market for their surpluses and therefore a way to stop losing money (surpluses drive down prices, causing a loss in income). Assuming that the two countries are friends and not foes, the rulers of both have good reasons to get together and to work out a trade deal.

Fundamental to wanting data on a population is appreciating the value of knowing this vs (versus) that number of things, such as able-bodied men and bushels of surplus wheat. Said appreciation existed at least 30,000 years ago and probably dates back farther than that. Evidence of it is seen in systematic notches cut 30,000 years ago into animal bones found here and there in Europe and the Middle East. They have been interpreted as symbols constituting records kept of observations made/data collected (e.g., the number of bison killed).

To this evidence may be added thousands of carefully made clay objects stumbled upon for decades at archaeological sites in Iraq, Syria, Turkey, Israel, and Iran. They were fire hardened/kiln dried, as opposed to sun dried, and thus wear-resistant; half an inch to two inches in size; inscribed with standardized patterns of lines; and mass produced in seven standardized shapes from 8000 to 4400 B.C. and in nine more from 4400 to 3500 B.C. (Rudgley, 1999, pp 48-57). Their purpose was a puzzle until the late 1980s, when these objects came to be seen as ingredients of a system for redistributing goods within and between communities. At that time, they began to be called counters and tokens. It is felt that their three-dimensional shapes gave rise to the two-dimensional shapes of the pictograms (stylized pictures) etched onto clay tablets in Sumer - southern Iraq - between 3400 and 3100 B.C. After 3100 B.C., Sumerian tablets with pictograms were replaced by tablets having wedge-shape inscriptions collectively termed cuneiform writing, a writing popular in Iraq and its surroundings from 3000 to 100 B.C. Deciphering the pictograms and cuneiform writing on Sumer's tablets revealed the tablets to be primarily records kept of business activities: sales, purchases, receipts, stock inventories, deeds, etc.

Approximately 1000 B.C. we see the start of and gradual rise in rulers of European and Middle Eastern countries who periodically order studies to be conducted to update what is known about their populations. Like notches on bones, like counters, and like some pictograms and cuneiform writing before them, the data collected were tallies, counts, frequencies, or enumerations and signified how often things of a certain kind (e.g., men, wheat) were observed. These studies aimed at observing *all* the things of a population and thus being complete enumerations, referred to as *censuses*. Studies aimed at observing *some* of the things of a population, Those in a population, those in a sample meant to mirror the population and thus being incomplete enumerations, are referred to as *surveys*. Hence a survey is to a sample what a census is to a population. Incidentally, the word survey is applied to parcels of land too, where its meaning is different. Surveys of samples or, as typically termed, sample surveys have been common in the U.S. for about eighty years. They were seldom done before 1940 because of distrust in the ability of a sample to reflect the population from which it was created. Misgivings over samples slowly faded as the *random* type of sample became better accepted. It was conceived in 1875 by Charles Peirce, a U.S. physicist, mathematician, logician, and philosopher.

Wars between nations that ended with one nation defeating another often led to a victorious country annexing one or more vanquished countries as vassals (vassal states, or provinces). If this was done, then the conquering nation would frequently conduct a census to get data on one or more of the nations it conquered. Such data were the basis for: levying taxes on residents of a subjugated (subject) nation, drafting young residents (subjects) into the victor's army; and identifying subjects possessing certain skills, like doctors, stonemasons, jewelers, miners, and shipbuilders. One of the earliest censuses inspired by conquest was that of Persia (now Iran). Persians conquered Babylonia, a kingdom in Mesopotamia (now Iraq), in 538 B.C.; toppled Egypt in 525 B.C.; and did censuses of both. Romans did 70 censuses between 435 B.C. and 35 A.D.

From 1500 onward, censuses by European countries were performed more often and got data on more kinds of things. The reason behind this was a critical stage reached in the political and economic growth of Europe's nations, a stage made possible by technological advances, social reforms, and escalating desire of countries and their citizens to realize their potentials. The result was four European developments: the Protestant Reformation (circa 1525), the Scientific Revolution (circa 1600), the Age of Enlightenment/Age of Reason (circa 1700), and the Industrial Revolution (circa 1800).

Satisfying the needs that modern nations have for data became an ever-pressing challenge after 1600 because of incessant changes inside them. This challenge forced countries to improve upon how they collect data and process data (convert data to information). Furthermore, it caused them to realize that censuses alone could no longer meet all their data needs. Besides a census commissioned every five to ten years, there must be ways to collect and process data at the time the events signified by these data happen. Realizing this led to implementing methods to regularly collect and process data and to regularly send processed data - information - to those needing it. Some additional data collection or processing would be done by a government. The rest was left to a nation's merchants, bankers, manufacturers, etc., who needed such supplementary data anyway in order to function properly.

Around 1675, there began to be interest in recording births, deaths, marriages, age at death, cause of death, and epidemics (their nature, date of onset, duration, locations, etc.). Said records were seen to provide a basis in data, a database, for identifying trends and making predictions that would be beneficial to a country's functioning. A major impetus to compiling records was a book the Englishman William Petty wrote in 1679 about what he termed political arithmetic. In it he offered insights regarding what to get data on and how to process data. His book got the ball rolling on collecting a rich variety of population data germane to a nation's functional integrity. The political arithmetic that Petty conceived became a field of endeavor lasting from 1700 to 1825 roughly. Now his book was inspired by a friend and fellow countryman, John Graunt. Graunt had published in 1662 tables summarizing as frequencies (counts) the voluminous unwieldy data contained in the English Bills of Mortality. As an aside, the words statistics and statistical were first used in a treatise by Sir John Sinclair, another Englishman, entitled. It was written about 1800 and employed statistics in its first sense, observations of human population characteristics (page 1).

Some of the best studies done in the 1700s to collect and process new, or reprocess old, data on populations were done in England. And some of the best thinking on how to improve the ways data are collected and processed was also English. However, notable studies and thinking along these lines took place elsewhere in Europe too, particularly in Germany. Two Germans stand out, Gottfried Achenwall and Johann Peter Süssmilch. In 1746, Achenwall commenced lecturing at Marburg on what he saw as useful vs useless sorts of population data and on where to find records containing the useful kinds. Those attending these lectures spread his ideas across Europe. Süssmilch was an important advocate of care in selecting and utilizing methods to calculate annuities and life insurance, a couple of fairly recent innovations. His methods relied on mortality-type population data. During the late 1700s, there started to spring up in the more progressive nations of Europe government bureaus whose staff maintained records of population data they or others in a country regularly collected or processed. Such statistics 'bureaus', however, didn't become commonplace until the mid 1800s.

Approximately 1800, there began to occur throughout Europe followed by the U.S. a transition from national economies based primarily on rural and agricultural ways of making a living to national economies based chiefly on urban and industrial livelihoods. Coinciding with the transition was an upsurge in capitalism, a reorientation in banking, and a mushrooming of commerce (trade) between nations. Newly industrialized countries found they had a greater need than before to routinely obtain data to monitor and thereby know the states of their now more intricate economies. Naturally most of these data addressed industry and commerce. Since data on economics imply the wellbeing of a nation and since 'nation', in Greek, is 'polis', economics data were soon called political (national) data. Hence, William Petty's insightful political arithmetic.

Statistics, as a field/profession, has two origins. One is the political arithmetic of Petty. The other is anthropometry. Anthropometry collects and processes anthropometric data, data on the physical characteristics of humans (e.g., arm length and scull capacity). Belgian mathematician and astronomer Lambert Adolphe Jacques Quetelet (pronounced "ketlay") became intrigued with anthropometry around 1825. During his spare time he measured and compared the chest size of Scottish soldiers, the height of French army officers, etc. and in so doing pioneered anthropometry.

Quetelet was fascinated by regularities discovered in the anthropometric measurements/ data he collected. Specifically, he found that they regularly varied the same way astronomical observations had lately been found to regularly vary, a way today known as the normal distribution and the bell curve. Normal distribution and bell curve are descriptive labels. Normal means regular: the way data vary that is termed normal is the normal way data vary or the way data normally vary. Bell curve means if data are plotted as points on graph paper and if adjacent plotted points are connected by drawing straight lines between them then these lines become a single line that is not only curved but resembles the shape of an old-fashioned church bell.

Around 1835, the approach to data that had characterized a by then defunct political arithmetic merged with the approach to data being taken by Quetelet. The result was a new field, statistics. From political arithmetic, statistics inherited the practice of using arithmetic-addition, subtraction, multiplication, division, and making ratios-to process data into information. And from Quetelet's approach, statistics inherited the practice of employing the distributions conceived by a branch of mathematics, probability theory, to make reasonable inferences about populations utilizing the data of samples created from these populations. The normal distribution of data which so fascinated Quetelet was the beginning of this distribution being, out of all the distributions conceived by probability theory, the most useful to statistics. Yet a few others proved useful too, especially one known as the binomial distribution. Incidentally, the distributions of probability theory are termed probability distributions and frequency distributions, since they address both probabilities (the probability such-and-such will happen) and frequencies (how frequently such-and-such did happen).

The relationship between statistics and probability theory initiated by Quetelet grew stronger as time passed. Indeed, both fields became like two peas in a pod once statistics joined probability theory as a branch of mathematics in about 1890. Thus, it would be good to take a look at probability theory.

Probability theory arose as a branch of mathematics around 1655. Its birth was not due to interest in knowing the characteristics of human populations. Rather, it was due to an interest in gambling which spread like wildfire across much of Europe in the 1500s and 1600s. Gambling was particularly popular in France and with aristocrats, who by wanting to get richer wanted to know as accurately as possible their chances of winning at games of chance. Now in the 1500s the chances, or likelihood, of an event happening on a play of a game (e.g., winning a soil of a roulette wheel) were called the odds in favor of, or favoring, the event. And the chances/likelihood of an event not happening were dubbed the odds against the event. In the 1600s, the likelihood/chances of an event occurring, or not occurring, commenced to be also known as the probability of the event's occurrence, or non-occurrence.

Odds and probabilities differ. Two numbers are used when giving the odds of an event occurring (e.g., the odds in favor of drawing a spade from a well shuffled deck of playing cards are 13 to 39, 13 being the number of spade cards and 39 being the number of non-spade cards in the deck). One number is used when citing an event's probability of occurrence (e.g., the probability of occurrence of drawing a spade from a well shuffled deck of playing cards is 0.25; found by dividing 13 by 52, 52 being 13 spade cards +39 non-spade cards and hence all deck cards). Likelihoods take the form of odds in games of chance where money is received or lost by players at the end of each play of a game. Likelihoods are expressed as probabilities in nearly all other situations.

Attempts to specify a player's chances in games of chance led to the insight that chance is not unpredictability, only much less predictability than desired. Out of this realization came probability theory, the branch of mathematics devoted to discovering and describing the regularities, orderliness, or lawfulness in chance happenings. The theory gave gamblers and others (e.g., insurance companies) ways to know and apply the laws of chance, technically called the laws of randomness. Probability theory stemmed from an exchange of letters in 1654 between two Frenchmen, the mathematician Pierre de Fermat and mathematician-physicist Blaise Pascal. In their letters they created the first of various laws of chance, laws of probability, or rules of probability. Other laws/rules would follow. One was set forth in 1705 by the Swiss mathematician Jacques Bernoulli. It allows us to state the probability of an event occurring in situations characterized as Bernoulli trials, or a Bernoulli process. Such a probability is found by consulting a probability distribution Bernoulli conceived, the binomial distribution. This distribution was the first of many probability distributions embodying probability theory.

We will end our digression into probability theory with the normal (probability) distribution. Unlike the binomial distribution, the normal distribution was conceived over a roughly eighty-year period and by three people: the French mathematician Abraham de Moivre (in 1733), French astronomer-mathematician Pierre Laplace (1778), and German mathematician-astronomer Carl Friedrich Gauss (1809). During the 1700s, astronomers increasingly assumed the things they observe and relationships between these things are regular occurrences. They further assumed that nature or, what came to mean the same thing, the universe operates much like a viable society does, by being orderly or lawful (law-abiding). Slight dispersion, variability, or deviations in their observations of the same thing (e.g., a star) were sometimes seen. It was passed off as individual differences among observers (e.g., this versus that astronomer's eyesight, telescope, or skill) and as slight differences in the same observer's mental keenness while observing the same thing on different occasions.

Gauss would refer to slight dispersion, variability, or deviations in astronomical observations as errors in observation. He thought that the normal distribution mirrors how these errors are distributed and consequently named it the law of error, or error law, and error curve. During the late 1800s it was renamed the Gaussian law (of error), Gaussian curve, and Gaussian distribution. In the early 1900s, the distribution was also called the normal law (of error). And since about 1950 it has usually gone by the names normal distribution, normal curve, and bell curve. Gauss' excitement over how nicely this distribution describes the dispersion in the errors of astronomical observations led Quetelet to use it for describing dispersion in anthropometric observations (page 5).

Social reform was in the wind in Europe and the U.S. during the mid and late 1800s. Into this wind was swept the newborn field of statistics, largely because of claims made by Quetelet. Around 1845, Quetelet said not only anthropometric-type data but all types of data on people are normally distributed. To know what he meant by this, we need to know what is meant by normally, normal, and a norm. A norm is a standard or reference point. Normal is an average which is treated as a norm/standard/reference point. And normally is the adverb of normal. So, what is meant by the statement that all types of data on people are normally distributed? Basically, it means all such data fall in roughly equal amounts to either side of the average calculated for a set of data, this average serving as a norm and signifying normal. Quetelet's claim that all types of data regarding people are normally distributed turned out to be largely correct, although initially it was doubted by many.

More controversial was his interpretation of data to either side of the average (to either side of what's normal). Gauss construed such data as imperfections in observing things and thus as *imperfect observations*. Quetelet saw them as imperfections in things observed and thus as *imperfect things*. Therefore, a thing (e.g., a person) is perfect in terms of some characteristic (e.g., height) if the thing does not differ from the average of this characteristic. Otherwise this thing is imperfect. Suppose the average height of adult men in the U.S. is 5'8". Quetelet would say 5'8" is the perfect height for adult American men and that all adult American men 5'8" tall are perfect, in height. All shorter than or taller than 5'8" are imperfect, in height. Now a person perfect in all characteristics-(height, weight, health, education, income, morality, etc.) is a perfect person. And a perfect person is an average person, a normal person, and a mediocre person.

As of 1845, Quetelet was a social activist. This is implied by his strong interest at that time in social and economic characteristics and his openly advocating that nations elevate to average socioeconomic status all citizens below average in health, education, and income. Quetelet's ideas were provocative, provoking debate on four fronts. One front were the pros and cons over government intervention in people's lives. Another was fear that economic disincentives would result from averaging out, or homogenizing, personal incomes. Still another front was the wisdom of concentrating on an average to the exclusion of the dispersion associated with it. Finally, a few thought much could be learned about people by concentrating on dispersion to the exclusion of its associated average, a stance that led during the late 1800s and early 1900s to the study in biology and psychology of individual differences.

Amid the hubbub about its social implications, statistics continued doing what political arithmetic had once done; namely, collect and process population data important to a country's functioning. From 1850 on, statistics evolved into a key tool and aspect of government, economics, and business. Breakthroughs came in making tables and graphs more informative, graphing trends, and creating price indexes (price index numbers). In the late 1800s, statistics started to be applied to areas within biology, initially heredity. Around 1890 it became a branch of mathematics, bringing it closer to probability theory. Shortly afterward, statistics began refining its concepts of average, dispersion, relationship, population, and sample. Also it began drawing heavily upon probability theory for developing concepts and techniques to use in making reasonable inferences about populations from the data in samples. Pioneers of a more mathematical statistics (1880-1910) were all English: Francis Edgeworth, Francis Galton, Karl Pearson, Udny Yule, Charles Spearman, William Gossett.

From its inception as a profession around 1835 until roughly 1910, statistics lacked a clear identity. The reason is that its identity was mainly the identity of the profession of which it was an aspect and for which it was the provider of tools meeting needs specific to said profession, be this profession economics, biology, psychology, education, etc. Thus, a statistician was often an economist (Edgeworth), biologist (Galton), psychologist (Spearman), or industrial chemist (Gossett) interested in applying statistics to his field of endeavor. An English economist, William Bowley, finished writing in 1901 a very early textbook on statistics, one having an economics slant. Frequently a profession regarded statistics as an important element making up a still larger aspect of this profession, an aspect which specializes in data collection or processing. Instances of these specialties are econometrics in economics, biometrics in biology, and psychometrics in psychology. Only after about 1910 did statistics' identity become clearer.

CHAPTER 2

THE NATURE OF STATISTICS

The last chapter gave a preliminary impression of what statistics is all about. In this chapter we will get a better impression. Let us begin by taking a look at the purpose of statistics. Its purpose is to tell us about a group of things (e.g., men) or a relationship between groups of things (e.g., men and women). Which means the purpose of statistics is not to tell us about a thing (e.g., Paul) or a relationship between things (e.g., Paul and Carol). Probability theory has the same purpose statistics has. Now it is their having a shared purpose which led me on page 6 to liken statistics and probability theory to two peas in a pod. This commonality is why it is not unusual to come across a textbook on probability (theory) and statistics.

Consequently this book deals with situations where interest is in a group of things, not in a thing of a group, and in a relationship between groups of things, not in a relationship between a thing in one group and a thing in another group. This is not to say we will be ignoring things. Far from it. We'll be up to our eyeteeth in them. However, our interest in things will be limited to treating them as means to an end. The end is to know a group of things or a relationship between groups of things. And the means for reaching this end is knowing the things in the group or, for a relationship between groups, knowing the things in two or more groups.

Before we leave the subject of distinguishing between knowing a group of things and knowing a thing it might be good to firm up the implications of this distinction with an illustration. Consider the group of Scottish soldiers whose chest size Quetelet measured and compared (page 5). We do not know how many he studied. Assume he only had time to study 200 soldiers. A group so small would be a sample, not the population, of Scottish soldiers. Assume, too, the 200 measurements made range from 36 inches through 48 inches.* If interest is in the group of soldiers, then interest is in all 200 chest measurements and in utilizing them to find the group's average chest size and its dispersion in chest size. Suppose the measurements are used to calculate average chest size and dispersion in chest size and that these two statistics - these two pieces of sample information (page 1) - are 42" and 6" respectively. Note that a 6" dispersion means 3" of dispersion to one side of the 42"

---

* Note that most data are measurements. A measurement is a number (e.g., 36) followed by a unit of measurement (e.g., inches).

average and 3" of dispersion to the other side of it. Further suppose that after plotting the measurements on graph paper we see that the resulting curve has a bell shape and hence is a normal distribution. By knowing the 200 measurements are normally distributed we can automatically say 68% of the soldiers have a chest size between 39" (42" – 3") and 45" (42" + 3"). Whereupon we can also say that 0.68 x 200 = 136 soldiers have a chest size from 39" to 45".

Implicitly, we are treating the above distribution as a frequency distribution. Thus, it gives us the frequency, count, or number of times the 200 measurements fell into one or another of, say, thirteen classes of chest sizes into which he classified them so as to get a bird's eye view of their dispersion. The chest sizes might be 36", 37", 38"------46", 47", and 48"; the frequencies associated with them might be 4,11,18--------19,11, and 2. We could treat this frequency distribution as a probability distribution. By doing so, we will know the probability, likelihood, or chances of meeting in the near future a soldier from the group, given we meet one, who has a chest size of such-and-such. However, we can know said probability only if whichever soldier we meet is met on a chance, or random, basis. Thus, our meeting him must be a random/chance occurrence/event in order for our likelihood of meeting any soldier of the group having such-and-such chest to be accurate. Now for a word of caution. To know that the occurrence of a thing is due solely to chance, to a roll of the dice so to speak, isn't as easy as it might seem and is rarely possible under everyday circumstances.

Statistics is interested in two kinds of groups, populations and samples. A population is a group of all things of a certain kind (e.g., all Scottish soldiers). A sample is a group of some things of a certain kind (e.g., some Scottish soldiers). Many samples can be created from a population. Each sample differs from every other insofar as the specific things in it. Statistics is primarily interested in populations. Yet almost never can we observe all things of a certain kind (a population). Nearly always we must resort to observing only some things of a certain kind (a sample). Just as knowing things is the way to know a sample, knowing a sample is almost always the only way to know a population. Hence statistics is secondarily interested in samples.

To the degree the things in a population selected to be things in a sample resemble things in the population not selected to be in the sample, then to that degree the sample is said to represent, mirror, reflect, or be representative of the population. The highest degree to which a sample represents, mirrors, reflects, or is representative of a population is attained when population things are chosen on a random basis to also be sample things. And the most accurate way of knowing if sample information is or is not essentially the same as population information is when population things are selected on a random basis to be sample things. Any sample whose things have been randomly picked from a population is known as a random sample. Of all the types of samples pieced together from population things, statistics is interested in random samples.

The process of creating, obtaining, drawing, piecing together, assembling, etc. samples from populations is termed sampling. A population from which one or more samples are drawn is referred to as the population sampled. Let's begin our discussion of sampling with an illustration. It involves a nonhuman population, to underscore the remark on page 1 that populations of things other than people exist too.

Consider the Whitman Sampler. The Whitman Sampler is a box of chocolate candies manufactured by Whitman. It gets its name from being a sample of these chocolates. Actually, the Whitman Sampler is many samples because many Samplers have been packaged over the years. Samplers come in small, medium, and large boxes. A small box contains roughly a dozen chocolates, a medium-size box around two dozen, and a large box approximately three dozen. The candies in every Sampler are chosen by the company with the intent that they mirror the assorted candies it makes. More precisely, every Sampler is so constituted as to represent the entire line of Whitman's chocolates (during a particular span of time), an entirety which defines the population of Whitman chocolates (for that time span).

The logic behind the Sampler is that we will think the population of chocolates is as good as we found the sample (Sampler) of chocolates to be. Our rating of the goodness of the Sampler comes from observing and hence seeing, tasting, smelling, and touching its chocolates. And our resulting observations take the form of data we collect on the amounts of pleasure we get from each chocolate's color, shape, size, taste, firmness, etc. From these data we next infer, or make an inference about, the population of Whitman chocolates. Such inferring leads us to buy/not buy Whitman chocolates in the future. All of this is done in our heads, without the aid of pencil and paper, calculator, or statistics. If we desire our inference to be more accurate, then we will need to observe more than merely one Sampler.

Let us build upon this illustration so as learn more about the nature of statistics. Consider two scenarios, one simple and the other complex. Both entail a procedure. The procedure for the simple scenario has four steps. First, we create a random sample. Assume it consists of five Samplers, in small boxes, we pick at random off a store shelf. Inasmuch as the Samplers are randomly selected, our sample is random. Thus our sample is representative of the population. Second, we eat two chocolates a day for a month. This means we consume roughly 60 chocolates in a month, because there are roughly 12 chocolates per Sampler and 12 x 5 = 60. Five minutes after eating a chocolate we record our impression of it: good, fair, bad.

Our hope is that the sample information (which is knowable) generated in the next step turns out, in the last step, to be essentially the same as population information (which isn't knowable). After completing the second step, we have sixty pieces of data. They are our sixty impressions of the sixty chocolates eaten. Third, we process the sample data (these sixty impressions), thereby transforming it into sample information. Fourth, we decide whether sample information is or is not essentially the same as population information.

This scenario leads to a more accurate inference about the population of Whitman chocolates. In fact, its inference would likely be much more accurate than we'd ever want. But that would not be true of a study conducted by the taste preference laboratory at Whitman, assuming Whitman has one. For the lab would regard the simple scenario as incapable of yielding an accurate inference. The reason why is that the lab is interested in more than your or my impressions of how tasty Whitman chocolates are. Which brings us to the complex scenario and into the realm of professional research. The lab would seek the impressions of people within a subpopulation of the U.S. population, a subpopulation known by market researchers to be more inclined to eat chocolates than the rest of the population. And the lab would design and perform a study which uses a random sample of at least thirty people drawn (selected) from the subpopulation. Lab researchers would consider this subpopulation to be their target subpopulation.

Whitman's lab would follow the complex scenario and its more intricate procedure. The study might be a survey but is more apt to be an experiment, a study done amid the fairly well controlled conditions (surroundings) offered by a laboratory. Many questions need to be answered while designing the study. Precisely what is the subpopulation of interest? How many people in this subpopulation ought to be sampled? The number picked, say 50, is the study's sample size. What is the best way to sample (get a sample from) the subpopulation? In what order are members of the sample to eat the chocolates being evaluated? These are some of the many questions to be asked.

Various types of samples are acknowledged, some random and others nonrandom. Random samples take three forms: simple random samples, stratified random samples, cluster samples. Nonrandom samples take many forms: systematic samples, systematic samples with a random start, stratified systematic samples, stratified systematic samples with a random start, convenience samples (ie, presenting samples, quota samples, and judgment samples). Most statistical techniques employed for inferring population information from sample information assume sample data come from simple random samples. If their assumption is not honored, then they produce inferences which can't be justified! Occasionally this assumption is met by systematic samples/stratified systematic samples having a random start. A few statistical techniques for inferring population information from sample information assume sample data come from either stratified random samples or cluster samples, since strata and clusters are simple random samples. Lastly, a sampling frame is a list of things in a population. Sampling frames are employed to create samples from populations whose members can all be identified.

It's time to see in detail at how statistics enables us to know a population by knowing a sample. Our discussion focuses on one type of sample, the simple random sample (SRS). Now after sample data are transformed into sample information a question must be asked and answered: are sample information and population information essentially the same? Two answers are possible. One is that they are essentially the same; the other is that they are significantly different. Unfortunately, the answer arrived at is not necessarily correct. It might be right. Or it might be wrong. The statistical technique used to generate sample information from sample data is not able to tell us whether we are certainly right or certainly wrong. But it is able to do the next best thing, give us the probability our answer is right or the probability our answer is wrong. So even though we cannot know for sure whether we're right or wrong we can know if we are probably right vs probably wrong. While this is far from what we would like, it is definitely better than nothing.

Sometimes we want sample and population information to be essentially the same. This is the case when we use sample information to estimate population information (e.g., to estimate the average medical costs of all adults in America during 2016, based upon knowing the average medical costs of some American adults in 2016). And if this is the case then we will want to know our confidence in saying that our population information estimate is essentially the same as our sample information. At other times we want sample information and population information to be significantly different. This happens when we hope to show that a sample we obtained from a population can no longer be regarded a sample from the population (because we did something to the sample before we commenced collecting data from it). And when this happens we will want to know our risk in saying our sample information is significantly different from population information (because the sample now represents a different population).

One step in the design stage of a study is the person doing the study specifying his desired level of confidence in saying sample information and population information are essentially the same or his desired level of risk in saying sample information and population information are significantly different. Level of confidence and level of risk are stated as percentages (e.g., 95% confidence and 5% risk). These percentages are based upon the probabilities (e.g., 0.95 and 0.05) making up probability distributions (e.g., the normal distribution). Statisticians see confidence and risk as being opposites. Also they see an inverse, or seesaw, relationship between levels of confidence and levels of risk. Thus the confidence levels 99%, 95%, or 90% typically adopted when estimating population information are the same as the risk levels 1%, 5%, or 10% typically adopted when determining the significance of a difference.

Statistics engages in two basic activities. One is describing samples and populations. The other is using samples to make inferences about populations. Therefore statistics is divided into two basic areas, descriptive statistics and inferential statistics. Descriptive statistics is concerned with concepts and techniques which pertain to transforming sample data into sample information and, if doable, transforming population data into population information. Of course, most of its activity is processing sample data into sample information, given that the population information we yearn to know is almost always impossible or unfeasible for us to know through processing population data (data collected from all things in a population).

Inferential statistics is concerned with concepts and techniques which pertain to transforming sample information into population information. Processing sample information into population information involves inferring that sample information and population information are, depending upon what interests us, essentially the same or significantly different. Thus inferential statistics is also concerned with specifying the criterion we adopt for deciding sample and population information are essentially the same/significantly different as well as with the confidence/risk level that dictates this criterion. Note that even though inferential statistics deals with inferences it also deals with descriptions. For the inferences it makes describe populations and are thus inferred descriptions, or inferential descriptions, of populations.

Inferential statistics has as its main interests the two interests its users normally have, estimating population information and determining significance of differences. Inferential statistics commonly employs a couple of terms we need to introduce. They are technical equivalents of what we've been calling sample information and population information. Sample information and population information are respectively termed statistics and parameters. Therefore, the two main interests of inferential statistics are estimating parameters - creating parameter estimates - and determining significance of differences.

The final thing required in learning the nature of statistics is knowing what statistics means by information. What is meant by sample information (statistics) and population. information (parameters)? As used in statistics, information is hard to define in a way that is meaningful. Back on page 1 we said information is either complex or relatively organized observations. However, that is the definition of information in its usual sense and is not quite what statistics has in mind. And to say that, in statistics, information is whatever is generated from sample data or population data leaves much to be desired. So we will not attempt a definition of statistical information. Instead we will identify the types of such information. Before doing this, it will be desirable to first look at how characteristics of things are classified.

The oldest classification divides characteristics into qualitative characteristics and quantitative characteristics. Qualitative characteristics have been increasingly referred to as categorical characteristics since the 1960s. A categorical/qualitative characteristic (e.g., ethnicity, or ethnic background) manifests itself in states thought of as categories that differ from each other in kind (e.g., Greek, Swedish, Angolan, Japanese, Mexican, Russian, and Iranian); a quantitative characteristic (e.g., temperature) exhibits states that differ from each other in amount (e.g., 50 degrees and 75 degrees Fahrenheit). A refinement in the classification was introduced around 1947 which is used in psychology and sociology. It refers to a categorical characteristic as a nominal characteristic and sees a quantitative characteristic as more precisely being an ordinal, interval, or ratio characteristic (depending on how its quantities differ from one another).

An ordinal characteristic (e.g., intelligence) has quantities we distinguish between only by saying one of them (e.g., an intelligence quotient-IQ-score of 120) is less than or greater than another (e.g., 110 or 140). Many psychological characteristics are ordinal, even though some may seem interval due to how they are defined. An interval characteristic has quantities we distinguish between by additionally saying one is less than or greater than another by such- and-such. And a ratio characteristic (e.g., weight) is an interval characteristic having a complete absence of quantity, which is symbolized by zero. Interval characteristics are mostly conveniences, created so we can more easily deal with states of some ratio characteristics. For instance, temperature is a ratio characteristic ordinarily treated as an interval characteristic. While the scales in terms of which temperature is commonly measured (the Fahrenheit scale and Celsius, or centigrade, scale) contain a zero (i.e., 0 degree Fahrenheit and 0 degree Celsius), the zero on them does not mean no temperature. Envisioned as an interval characteristic, temperature has quantities (temperatures) we can distinguish between by saying that one of them (e.g., 50 degrees Fahrenheit) is less than or greater than another (e.g., 75 degrees) by such-and-such (25 degrees).

Eight types of statistical information are commonly employed in statistics. They are identified and defined below:

1. Frequencies: A frequency, or count, is the number of times a particular state (e.g., male) of a particular characteristic (i.e., sex) of a group (e.g., historians living in Texas) was observed (e.g., 10). By a group is meant, here and in what follows, a sample or a population. Also, a frequency is the number of times (e.g., 5) an event (e.g., 'false-positive") associated with a group (e.g., the outcomes of administering a certain medical test) was observed. Event is a term often used in probability theory. It means the occurrence of a state of a categorical/nominal characteristic,

2. Frequency Distributions: A frequency distribution is a portrayal of frequencies of states of a particular characteristic (e.g., sex) of a group (e.g., historians living in Texas), each frequency referring to a particular state (e.g., male) of the characteristic. If the characteristic is quantitative, its frequencies are arrayed and hence made into an array. By an array is meant the quantities of a quantitative characteristic (an ordinal, interval, or ratio characteristic) are arranged into a series that, when looked at from left to right, either steadily increases in size (e.g., 34, 38, 41, 49, 55, 70) or steadily decreases in size (e.g., 70, 55, 49, 41, 38, 34). A frequency distribution also is a portrayal of the frequencies of events (e.g., false-positive, false-negative, true-positive, true-negative) associated with a group (e.g., the outcomes of administering a certain medical test). Frequency distributions can take the form of a table of frequencies - frequency table - or the form of a graph, in which frequencies are depicted either as bars (i.e., a bar graph or a histogram) or as lines drawn between plotted points (i.e., a line graph that here is more precisely termed a frequency polygon, since its shape is that of a polygon).

3. Relative Frequencies: A relative frequency (e.g., 0.10), a commonly encountered kind of proportion, is a frequency (e.g., 10) of a state that's been made relative to, or thus been divided by, all frequencies (e.g., 100) of states of a particular characteristic (e.g., sex) of a group (e.g., historians living in Texas). Also, a relative frequency (e.g., 0.02) is the frequency (e.g., 5) of an event (e.g., false-positive) which is relative to all frequencies (e.g., 250) of events (e.g., false-positive, false-negative, true-positive, true-negative) associated with a group (e.g., outcomes of administering a certain medical test). Relative frequencies of states of a particular characteristic of a group or of events - occurrences-associated with a group can, like frequencies, be portrayed via a frequency distribution. When this is done, the frequency distribution is sometimes called a relative frequency distribution. Now, as for employing the words proportion and relative frequency, there are times one is preferred over the other. We'll treat both words as the same.

Notice that a relative frequency provides an often desirable perspective on the frequency underlying it by showing where that frequency stands in relation to all the frequencies constituting the frequency distribution for the group being considered. For instance, the relative frequency 0.02 indicates that the frequency underlying it (which may be any one out of many frequencies, but above was 5) is very small, compared to all frequencies. Notice, too, that an easier to grasp number results from multiplying a relative frequency by 100, converting it into a percentage. Thus, by multiplying the relative frequency 0.02 by 100, we get the percentage 2%. However, doing this when the sum of all frequencies for a group totals less than fifty is deceptive since percent or, more accurately, per cent means per one hundred and consequently signifies a basis (reference point) of one hundred separate numbers (Blalock, 1979, pp 33-34). Which is why it's a good practice to give along with a percentage the sum of the frequencies, the 'base', used for calculating its associated proportion (the sum 250, in the above example). My advice for what to do when you see a percentage is this. If the base cited for it is much less than fifty (e.g., forty), be wary of what it says it is indicating. And if its base is not cited then ignore it.

4. Averages: An average is the typical state of a frequency distribution or in other words, the typical state exhibited by a characteristic of a group. Also an average is the typical event of a frequency distribution. Statistically minded people speak of central tendency instead of average, though we'll use the more popular word average. Average, or central tendency, can be expressed in various ways. Each of these ways is regarded a measure of average (central tendency). The major measures of average are the arithmetic mean and the median. Minor measures include the weighted arithmetic mean, the mid-range, the mode, the harmonic mean, and the geometric mean.

A couple of things should be pointed out. First, the arithmetic mean is, by far, the most commonly utilized average. Therefore, it's often called in everyday and even in technical discussions the average (e.g., the average annual rainfall in Boston is such-and-such) rather than the mean, and the mean rather than the arithmetic mean. This is fine, as long as people coming across the terms average and mean know exactly what's meant by them. Second, the different kinds of averages exist because each portrays average (typicality) better under certain circumstances than under others. Examples of such circumstances are whether a characteristic is interval/ratio vs ordinal, whether a characteristic's frequency distribution is bell-shaped vs skewed (lopsided), and whether in a specific situation some states of an interval/ratio characteristic ought to exert more influence-(carry more weight)-than others in determining the arithmetic mean in that situation.

5. Dispersions: A dispersion, variability, scatter, or spread is the extent of variation or change in states displayed by a characteristic of a group. Also a dispersion is the extent of variation in events of a frequency distribution. Dispersion, like average, can be expressed in various ways. Each of them is regarded a measure of dispersion. The major measures of dispersion are the standard deviation, the variance, the quartile deviation (semi-interquartile range), and the coefficient of variation. Minor measures include the range, the average deviation, the variation ratio (Blalock, 1979, p 76), and the index of qualitative variation (Mendenhall et al., 1974, p 121). Seldom are dispersions of interest in their own right. Rather, interest in dispersions is ordinarily for employing them to gauge how much stock we ought, or ought not, to place in the averages associated with them. Hence a dispersion bestows meaning on and thus establishes the usefulness of an average: the more dispersion in states of a characteristic, the less meaningful and useful the average state of that characteristic!

6. Differences: The commonly sought differences are those between frequencies, between proportions, between sets of ranks, between averages (mainly arithmetic means), and between dispersions (mainly variances). Ranks are numbers assigned quantities manifested either by an ordinal characteristic or by an interval/ratio characteristic treated as an ordinal characteristic. Thus, no more can sensibly be said about two different ranks (ranked quantities) than that one of them is less than or greater than the other. A set of ranks normally has its constituent ranks ordered (arrayed), usually from smallest to largest. The term rank-order signifies a set of ranks whose constituent ranks have been ordered (arrayed). Differences between two or more sets of ranks are, to be more precise, differences between two or more sets of ordered ranks or, put another way, differences between two or more rank-orders.

Most research studies are designed around calculating differences between frequencies, relative frequencies, sets of ranks, averages, or dispersions in the hope of discovering relationships between characteristics. Those of these studies that are experiments specifically hope to discover causal relationships between them.

7. Correlations: A correlation, also known as an association, is the *strength* of the relationship between states exhibited by one characteristic (e.g., height) and states displayed by one or more other characteristics (e.g., weight) of a group (e.g., U.S. adults). The reason

for italicizing the word strength is to stress correlation is not just another word for relationship. Rather, correlation is strength of relationship. The strength of a relationship ranges anywhere from very, very weak (essentially no relationship) to very, very strong (essentially a perfect relationship).

Correlation can be expressed in various ways. Each way is regarded a measure of correlation and is usually termed a coefficient of correlation, or a correlation coefficient. The major measure of correlation is the Pearson product-moment correlation coefficient (occasionally called 'the' correlation coefficient, which breeds confusion). Minor measures include Spearman's rank-order correlation coefficient, the Cramér statistic/coefficient, the correlation ratio (also referred to as 'eta'), the point-biserial correlation coefficient, the Pearson product-moment multiple correlation coefficient, the Pearson product-moment partial correlation coefficient, and Goodman and Kruskal's gamma. Besides these measures of correlation, which specify correlation by a number (typically from 0.00 through 1.00, indicating no through perfect correlation), correlation can be seen in the density and configuration of points plotted on graph paper that comprise a graph known as a scatter diagram, scattergram, or scatter plot. But this graphical, as opposed to numerical, method can only be employed for showing correlations between two interval/ratio characteristics. Moreover, it cannot be utilized to make trustworthy inferences.

It is very important to not confuse correlation with causation! Correlation is the degree to which states manifested by one characteristic coincide with states manifested by one or more other characteristics. Causation is the degree to which the states manifested by one characteristic are caused by/due to states manifested by one or more other characteristics. Yet correlation and causation are related: an at least moderate correlation (a moderately strong relationship) must exist in order for causation to be justifiably said to exist and thus for a relationship to be legitimately deemed causal. However, moderate correlation (i.e., 0.41 through 0.60 roughly), even perfect correlation (i.e., 1.00), can and does exist without causation also existing. An at least moderate correlation is necessary, but not sufficient (enough), for the existence of causation and therefore a causal relationship. Thus, we conclude that causation presupposes at least moderate correlation but even perfect correlation does not presuppose causation. Simply put, correlation and causation are not the same thing.

8. Regression Equations: A regression equation describes a relationship between quantities displayed by an interval/ratio characteristic (e.g., height) and quantities or categories exhibited by one or more other characteristics (e.g., weight) of a group (e.g., American adults). Creating a regression equation is worthwhile only if the relationship it is to describe is at least strong, as evidenced by one or more high correlations (strong relationships) between the two or more characteristics constituting it.

CHAPTER 3

UNIVARIATE, BIVARIATE, AND MULTIVARIATE ANALYSIS

Processing data into information is analyzing data. Thus, data processing and data analysis are the same thing. Analysis means separating, dissecting, or teasing apart data, followed by rearranging these data. Data analysis/data processing utilizes mathematical techniques. If the techniques are statistical, then data analysis is called statistical analysis. Statistical analysis can take place at three levels of complexity: univariate, bivariate, multivariate. Univariate statistical analysis analyzes data regarding one characteristic of a sample or one characteristic of a population, a characteristic of each thing in the sample or population. Bivariate (statistical) analysis processes data on two sample characteristics or two population characteristics. Multivariate analysis analyzes data pertaining to three or more characteristics. Variate means a characteristic that is treated as a variable. And a variable is a characteristic whose variation, changes in state, or changes in how it manifests, displays, or expresses itself is what a researcher wishes to know. Variable is a research term. Outside a research setting, characteristics are normally called characteristics and not variables. We'll use the terms characteristic and variable interchangeably in what follows.

From 1850 onward, statistics increasingly became a tool of government officials (statistics bureaus), economists, and businessmen. All three sought data concerning the population of their country. Initially the data they analyzed were population data, not sample data. By 1900, sample data were also being analyzed, thanks to promotion of random sampling by statistically minded economists in the 1890s. Analyses prior to 1900 were marginally statistical because statistics had little to offer yet in the way of techniques, all of the very few available being geared to univariate data analyses. More sophisticated statistical techniques and concepts began to appear from approximately 1900 on, chiefly in England.

This new wave in concepts and techniques greatly improved the caliber of univariate analyses and paved the way for bivariate and multivariate analyses. However, it was not until about 1915 that these concepts and techniques commenced being fairly well known and understood by economists and businessmen. Not until approximately 1930 did they start to be generally known and understood by biologists, educators, psychologists, and others. And as all of this was happening, statistics was slowly acquiring its identity as a distinct field of endeavor (page 9).

Economists during the late 1880s began to more accurately describe how the states manifested by economic characteristics (e.g., prices) of things (e.g., commodities) vary with the passing of time or, in other words, vary as a function of time. They did this by constructing price indexes and learning which of the measures of average (e.g., means vs weighted means vs medians vs geometric means) are best at revealing trends. They also did it by graphing moving averages - ordinarily moving means - of time series. Now a time series is a series (string) of events over a span of time. A moving average smooths out, or reduces, the jaggedness characterizing a curve in a time series graph, a jaggedness which makes it difficult to clearly spot trends nestled within the curve. In about 1900, economists started to make univariate statistical inferences that were parameter estimates and significance determinations.

A popular univariate inference was estimating the (arithmetic) mean of a population. To be accurate and to implement his level of confidence, an individual estimating a population mean has to calculate two things from his sample data. One is the sample mean. The other is the standard deviation of a probability distribution referred to as the sampling distribution of the mean. The standard deviation of the sampling distribution of the mean or, equivalently, the standard deviation of the mean is called the standard error of the (arithmetic) mean. It was conceived and first applied to observations in astronomy by Pierre Laplace, met on page 7.

We need to clarify a few things. First, there are many sorts of standard errors. Each is named after and specified in terms of a statistic: a sample mean, proportion, correlation, etc. (e.g., the standard error of the mean). Second, each is the standard deviation of a statistic (not of observations/data/measurements). Third, a probability distribution showing the dispersion/variability/deviations in a statistic is called the sampling distribution of that statistic. It is created by obtaining hundreds of simple random samples from an imaginary population of things. Fourth, sampling distributions employ test statistics. A test statistic (e.g., chi-square, t, F) is a statistic that allows us to estimate parameters and determine significant differences. Fifth, a few probability distributions, like the normal and binomial distributions, double as sampling distributions. Sixth, the error in standard error reminds us of what statisticians think of dispersion (page 7), particularly when they make inferences.

Seventh, after being used awhile to estimate parameters, standard errors began to be used to find significant differences. Initial interest was in the significance of the difference between a statistic, ordinarily a sample mean or sample proportion, and a number. The number was a parameter (e.g., a population mean or population proportion). But it functioned as a criterion/standard/reference point (e.g., no more than 0.02, or 2%, of all beef cattle purchased by a meat-packing company are to be discarded as unfit). These data analyses were univariate and involved conducting one-sample significance tests. A significance test is a statistical technique for testing/evaluating/assessing the significance of a difference.

Now the normal distribution is applicable only to interval/ratio characteristics (page 17) from which thirty, preferably forty, or more pieces of data have been collected. And the binomial distribution is applicable only to characteristics that manifest no more than two states, say male vs female or loud vs not loud. Hence as of 1900 many data had no distribution upon which to base inferences. The situation would soon be worsened by a growing stream of data on ordinal characteristics pouring out of psychological research. Analyzing data from these characteristics was problematic. If data were numbers, then referring statistics calculated with them to the normal distribution was thought by some to be of dubious validity. And if data were words specifying more than two states (e.g., low vs medium vs high motivation) then no statistic calculated with them would be compatible with the normal or the binomial distribution.

The mystique which came to surround the normal distribution in about 1815 started crumbling around 1885 under the weight of mounting evidence that, despite its accurately describing dispersion in the data of upwards to 90% of the interval/ratio characteristics studied, the distribution could no longer be seen the way Quetelet had seen it, as being an accurate description of the dispersion in all interval/ratio characteristics. From 1885 on, the normal distribution was less often termed the error law, Gaussian law, or normal law, since the word law in this context implies 100% applicability. Old habits die hard. It was not until roughly 1950 that textbooks generally replaced these names with the name normal distribution. Now economists, sociologists, and others familiar with statistics in the 1890s knew the normal distribution's shortcomings. Some of them even worked on inventing new probability distributions (e.g., sampling distributions).

About 1895, Karl Pearson identified a dozen types of probability/frequency distributions to which data from interval/ratio characteristics can be referred. These Pearsonian frequency curves, as they were called, would be mind boggling to all except the mathematically adept user of statistics, even the simplest curves (the Type 3, which include the normal distribution). Since such users were in the minority, the curves were not utilized much. They were seldom heard of after 1945. A byproduct of Pearson's work on probability distributions was a general technique he devised in 1900 for assessing how well a frequency distribution of data conforms to one of his frequency curves. This technique evolved into two specific techniques for determining significance, the chi-square test of goodness of fit and the chi-square test of independence.

Chi is pronounced ki, as in kite. It's the test statistic in the chi-square sampling distribution and is calculated from sample data using either of the above two chi-square tests. Both are one-sample significance tests for determining the significance of sample frequencies and relative frequencies of categories of one nominal characteristic (goodness of fit) or two nominal characteristics (independence). The first mentioned is univariate and the second bivariate. Occasionally either test is applied to an ordinal characteristic whose quantities have been categorized and thus resemble categories.

Pearson's interest and thoroughness in describing frequency/probability distributions, correlation, and regression set the stage for what would from 1910 to 1950 be fashionable in statistical analysis. Skimming statistics textbooks which appeared between 1915 and 1955 reveals a goodly amount of space that was typically devoted to indoctrinating readers in the new fashion by talking about: measures of average, dispersion, a frequency distribution's lopsidedness (skewness), a frequency distribution's peakedness (kurtosis), simple correlation (correlation of two characteristics), partial correlation (simple correlation, with the unwanted influence of a third, fourth, or even fifth characteristic controlled/neutralized), multiple correlation (correlation of three or more characteristics), simple regression (regression equations for two characteristics), multiple regression (regression equations for three or more characteristics).

Fashions change, and the foundation for things that would next be in vogue was laid down from 1920 to 1940. Its founders continued the English tradition (page 9). Chief among them were Ronald Fisher, Jerzy Neyman, and Egon Pearson, son of Karl Pearson. But about 1930, England had to begin sharing the statistics limelight with America. For that's around when George Snedecor and Louis Thurstone got into the act.

The chi-square goodness of fit and independence tests were the start of a long line of univariate, bivariate, and eventually multivariate inferential techniques for determining the significance of differences. In the 1940s, they began to be called significance tests. During the 1960s, they started also being termed hypothesis tests. Significance test was the name given to them by Fisher. Hypothesis test originated with Neyman and Egon Pearson, whose hypothesis testing approach was an extension of Fisher's significance testing approach. Now when in the early 1890s Pearson commenced making statistics mathematically respectable there was little in the way of what today are known as, with equal correctness, significance tests and hypothesis tests. The only significance test in common use was the 'z-test' employed to determine the significance of one mean (i.e., the significance of the difference between a sample mean and a performance standard). It utilized the standard error of the mean and was probably created by Laplace. During the next thirty years, the z-test evolved into a more general technique which wound up taking several specific forms, primarily the z-tests for one sample mean, one (sample) proportion, two means, and two proportions. Back in 1895, however, the z-test took only the first form.

The z-test, in any form, has a drawback. It can be applied only if the data in a situation are relatively numerous and consequently the sample(s) in that situation are relatively large. By relatively numerous and relatively large is meant that at least thirty, preferably forty, observations (data) are collected or, equivalently, that there are at least thirty things in each sample studied. Hence, a minimum of sixty data and things are required in order to use a z-test for determining the significance of the difference between two sample means or two sample proportions. Thirty, even sixty, pieces of data are not usually thought by statisticians to be very challenging. Of course that is today, a time characterized by routinely doing calculations electronically with minicomputers and personal computers. This was not the typical case before about 1965. Calculations prior to then were still often done electromechanically with desk calculators (e.g., the Monroe or the Marchant) and a set of mathematical tables.

Parenthetically, z is the symbol for z-score, or standard score, and standard score is a standard deviation unit. Standard scores are employed to specify degrees of dispersion in the *standard normal probability distribution*, which is what we have been calling the normal distribution. When you see 'z' in statistics or probability theory, automatically think 'normal probability distribution'. The rationale for referring the z calculated in a z-test to the normal distribution is this. If the size of a sample utilized in determining the significance of a sample mean or proportion or a difference between two sample means or proportions is at least thirty, then three things are assured. First, the sampling distribution of this mean or proportion or this difference between means or proportions is essentially normal. Second, the calculated z is essentially the same as the z corresponding to it in the (standard) normal distribution. Third, we know that the level of risk which *actually* exists is essentially the same as the risk level we desire.

If a person were to employ a z-test often, then he would have the incentive to devise an easier test. An alternate significance test was invented in 1908 by William Gossett, an English chemist working at Guinness brewery in Ireland. His work entailed him repetitively obtaining samples of a yeast culture to monitor its quality, so as to maintain the quality of beer brewed using the culture. Gossett not only invented a significance test to do this but a sampling distribution to which the test statistic calculated could be referred. They were dubbed the t-test, t distribution, and t-test statistic. Like the first form of the z-test, the t-test was for determining the significance of one mean. It was later able to also determine the significance of the difference between two means. Unlike the z-test it cannot determine the significance of proportions. Guinness allowed Gossett to publish his ideas on statistics, but only under a pen name (a fictitious name). The pen name he adopted was Student. Hence the origin of the names Student's t-test, t distribution, and t-test statistic. Gossett's t-test was little known until 1950, after which it became very popular.

The t-test was the earliest inferential technique applicable to small samples, though it can be applied to large samples too. In statistical analysis, a large sample has thirty or more things and a small sample has less than thirty things. Now until around 1920 there was the prevailing opinion that a random sample must contain a bare bones minimum of fifty things in order for the person doing a significance determination to have an acceptable level of risk. Which is why Pearson chided Gossett for relying on small samples. The basis for the above opinion was the frequent adoption of a very low level of risk, 1% or less, and a lack of consensus on how large a sample is needed to attain that risk level. Many carried to an extreme the rule of thumb: the larger the sample, the lower the risk. The result was the fairly widespread practice, before 1920, of using a z-test only if there were about a hundred things in a sample.

Now is a good time to clarify the word independence, as it is used by statisticians. Independence pertains to samples and to observations/data/measurements. All inferential statistical techniques assume a sample is independent. By this is meant that picking a thing in a population to also be in a sample has no effect on picking other things in the population to be in the sample. Most inferential statistical techniques assume observations, too, are independent. By this is meant a thing in a sample is observed no more than once during a given study (e.g., a study to find out if a relationship exists between accidents and cellphone usage). Observations exhibiting independence are called independent observations. A few inferential statistical techniques assume observations are dependent/related observations. I can only give a feel here for what is meant by related/dependent observations. The reason is that they are arrived at in two ways not readily grasped by a person unfamiliar with designing studies.

The value of related observations is they allow a researcher to control/neutralize the unwanted effect/influence of one or more variables/characteristics on the variable(s) being observed. Partial correlation (page 24) allows him to do the same; after, instead of while, observations are made. One way to accomplish such control is to observe a thing in a sample twice and thereby make two observations of it, the first before and the second after the thing is exposed to a situation/condition/treatment occurring in a study (e.g., observing the blood pressure of people with hypertension before and after they are given a certain blood pressure medicine). The two observations/data/measurements are related/dependent, since both are related to/dependent upon the same thing. Now the other way to achieve control is by splitting a sample into two or more groups/subsamples prior to observing things in it. This is done in a manner that results in these groups becoming mirror images of one another regarding the influence to be controlled.

Independent observations are made, in a study calling for them, through the use of two protocols. One is observing no more than once each thing/member of the study's sample(s) or the study's subsamples/groups. Not doing so wreaks havoc on the soundness of inferences made, which are flawed by flawed data collected and analyzed. And not doing it destroys the benefits obtained from getting a random sample. This situation plagued some users of the chi-square test of independence until word got out, about 1950, that its assumption of independent observations was being violated by them observing a person (employing the same person's data) two or more times in a study. As an aside, independence may be undermined by discarding, for whatever reason, one or more data collected. The other protocol is used when a sample is split into two or more groups. It stipulates that things in the sample are to be assigned on a random basis to these groups. This is what's meant by the term random assignment.

Another term worth knowing is bias. Bias is a systematic unwanted influence. It is also referred to as systematic error and nonrandom error, systematic being the opposite of random. Statisticians view the overall error in an observation as always consisting of random error and maybe consisting of systematic/nonrandom error too. Random error is unavoidable but specifiable and, by increasing sample size, reducible. Systematic error is largely avoidable, being that it can usually be prevented through properly designing a study. Research strives to acquire unbiased observations/data/measurements. Sources of unwanted influence, be it random or systematic, are referred to as extraneous variables/lurking variables/nuisance variables.

During the 1930s, univariate analysis took a backseat to bivariate analysis as interest swung from describing a characteristic in isolation to describing the strength and details of its relationship with another characteristic. There was interest in multivariate analysis also, but doing it was a formidable task in the day of electromechanical calculators. Determining the correlation/strength of a multivariate relationship composed of three or four variables required doing a slew of calculations before ever actually calculating a Pearson product-moment multiple correlation coefficient: calculating numerous sums, squares, sums of squares, and sums of cross-products. Just as intimidating were the calculations preliminary to calculating the Pearson product-moment partial correlation coefficient for determining the correlation of a bivariate relationship, after the unwanted influences of one or more extraneous variables are controlled/neutralized. Only a few people engaged in such grueling tasks, occasionally. Very few did so routinely.

The last two important developments in univariate analysis took place about 1930. Both addressed parameter estimates. A parameter estimate can take two forms, a point estimate and an interval estimate. A point estimate is one number, a statistic, while an interval estimate is two numbers, the upper limit and lower limit of an interval assumed to contain a parameter. The parameters estimated are typically population means and population proportions. Now one development was Ronald Fisher's criteria on what constitutes a good statistic for making parameter estimates. We won't discuss them. The other was Jerzy Neyman's technique for making more precise interval estimates. Interval estimates made with it are confidence interval estimates. Since 1970, these estimates have increasingly been called just interval estimates, because since then few other techniques have been routinely used to make interval estimates.

A point estimate is the only parameter estimate possible if a person knows nothing more than a statistic (e.g., a sample mean). Interval estimates are possible if a person knows a statistic and the data used to calculate it. The problem with point estimates is they cannot tell the person making them how confident he can be when saying a statistic (sample information) is essentially the same as a parameter (population information), something very desirable to know. People who make interval estimates have more confidence about this. And people making confidence interval estimates display still more confidence.

On page 22 we said economists began about 1900 to make parameter estimates and significance determinations. Their parameter estimates quickly went from being point estimates (e.g., a population mean is essentially the same as a sample mean) to being interval estimates (e.g., a population mean lies between the upper and lower limits of an interval defined by the standard error of the mean, the confidence being such-and-such). When mentioning his interval estimate (e.g., the mean duration of a labor strike is 15 days) an economist would also mention the standard error (e.g., 3 days). Increasingly these interval estimates were set forth thusly: the parameter is 15 ± 3 (i.e., the interval extends from $15 + 3 = 18$ to $15-3 = 12$), the confidence in this being 95%.

We finish this discussion of parameter estimates with an illustration of a confidence interval estimate. Consider a hypothetical survey of the eating habits of seventh graders in Louisiana. A report on findings of the survey says 'the 95% confidence interval for the mean daily intake of calories by seventh graders in Louisiana is 2000 to 2600'. The upper and lower confidence limits - 2600 and 2000 - and sample mean were calculated from data collected in the survey. Note that the middle of the confidence interval, 2300, is the point estimate of the mean daily intake of calories and that 2300 ± 300 is another way of expressing the confidence interval, 2600 to 2000.

In the decade preceding the above developments in parameter estimation, Fisher was pioneering a versatile technique for determining the significance of differences between means by analyzing the variances associated with them. This technique is the analysis of variance, or ANOVA. It was created for use in experiments and therefore in situations where most things that could exert unwanted influence on things observed are controlled through randomization primarily and matching secondarily. The technique is employed to discover and describe causal relationships between characteristics of things. Causal relationships may be bivariate or multivariate. So, too, may the analysis of variance. If an ANOVA is bivariate, it is called simple ANOVA; if multivariate, it is termed complex ANOVA. Notice we are encountering terminology similar to that used with chi-square, correlation, and regression: simple vs complex chi-square, simple vs multiple correlation, simple vs multiple regression.

No experiment arises magically. Time goes into thinking about its purpose (what it is to accomplish), designing it, settling on its procedures and its equipment, figuring out its cost, etc. before reaching the stage of doing it. Yet the designing of experiments was not considered a subject area by researchers until the appearance of the ANOVA. In the 1920s, Fisher identified around a dozen generic/general/basic designs of experiments to which his ANOVA could be applied. More experimental designs would be identified by him and others in the years to come. A researcher wishing to use ANOVA must decide which of these experimental designs to adopt in a study, since the experimental design adopted dictates how data are to be collected and processed into information. Which means the researcher will mull over the pros and cons of adopting this vs that design. In order to make a good decision, the researcher needs to know the purpose of her experiment and all experimental designs relevant to that purpose. The design settled on will largely determine the information obtained about the relationship between the two or more characteristics of interest (i.e., a study's study variables).

Many ANOVA experimental designs exist. The better known ones are the completely randomized design (one-way analysis of variance) and randomized block design (two-way analysis of variance) used in simple analysis of variance and the four factorial designs employed in complex analysis of variance: the completely randomized factorial, randomized block factorial, Latin square completely confounded factorial, and split-plot/block-treatment confounded factorial designs. The variables (characteristics of things) in a design are subdivided into study variables and extraneous variables. Study variables are subdivided into one or more independent variables and one dependent variable. An independent variable is an assumed cause in a causal relationship hoped to be discovered or is a known cause in a known causal relationship needing to be further described. All variables except the dependent variable are control variables, meaning they are under the control of a researcher (how well controlled, is another matter). Control variables are subdivided into independent variables and extraneous/lurking/nuisance variables (i.e., variables not in the relationship studied that will or might hinder knowing the relationship if their unwanted influence is not controlled/neutralized). A researcher controls an independent variable by manipulation or selection, by which is meant manipulating it to make it exist in certain states or selecting states in which it already exists. Extraneous variables are controlled by means of randomization or matching.

A few comments on terminology are needed. First, randomization is also known as random assignment, since it means assigning on a random basis, at random, or randomly the things in a sample to two or more groups created from the sample. Second, in experimental research an independent variable is sometimes termed a factor; a state of an independent variable is sometimes called an experimental condition, factor level, treatment level, or treatment; and a state of the dependent variable is sometimes termed a treatment effect. Third, in non-experimental research (e.g., survey research) an independent variable is frequently called a predictor variable, because it is the basis for making predictions; the dependent variable is often termed the predicted variable or response variable; and a state of the dependent variable is called a prediction.

Before getting into how the significance of differences between means is determined in the analysis of variance, we must understand why significant differences between two or more statistics - frequencies, proportions, ranks, averages, etc. - imply the existence of a relationship between characteristics. *All data collected* in a study that attempts to find a significant difference between two or more statistics *are data on one characteristic* in a relationship of interest, this characteristic being represented by the *study's dependent variable* or *(DV)*. In addition, this study has at least one other characteristic which exists in at least two states, the study's independent variable(s) or IV(s). Now a relationship, hopefully causal, between the IV(s) and DV is likely to exist if a significant difference is found between the two or more statistics calculated using data from the DV.

We should also remark on names given significance tests. A few are named after their test statistics: chi-square test, z-test, t-test, F-test. Some are named after their inventors: Friedman test, McNemar test, Cochran test. Others are named after what they analyze: signs (sign test), runs (runs test), variance (analysis of variance). Still others are a blend of the above practices: Wilcoxon rank-sum test, Mann-Whitney U test, Wilcoxon signed ranks test.

Analysis of variance analyzes variances (dispersions in data) associated with means in order to determine the significance of differences between these means. The ANOVA does this by first partitioning, subdividing, or splitting the variances into their component variances, their sources, or simply their causes. ANOVA's need and ability to tease specific causes of variance apart are why its experimental designs are the way they are. Next, one or more ratios of two component variances are created, one ratio in the case of simple and two or more ratios in the case of complex ANOVA. Then the quotient of the ratio(s) is calculated. It is a test statistic that went unnamed until 1934, which is when George Snedecor, a great admirer of Fisher, named it and its sampling distribution 'F' in his honor. Lastly, the significance of the calculated F(s) - the above quotient(s) - is determined by comparing its value with that of the appropriate F in the F distribution. If the calculated F is significant, then the difference between the two variances in it (those in the numerator and denominator of the above ratio) is judged to be significant. This indicates the differences between the three or more means associated with the variance in the ratio's numerator are also, *as a whole,* significant. The reason for italics is to stress that among the three or more differences between means there may be one or more, even two or more, which are not significant.

Snedecor was a professor at Iowa State University who became interested in statistics in 1914 and commenced applying it to agricultural research data around 1924. His early statistical work centered on multiple correlation and regression and on designing punch card machines to quickly categorize data collected. Snedecor and Fisher had two things in common, statistics and agricultural research. Fisher applied statistics to agricultural research data from 1919 to 1933, when he oversaw the research at Rothamsted (agricultural) Experimental Station. Snedecor invited Fisher to visit his university in 1931 to orient researchers and students there to the then barely known analysis of variance, after which he championed its use in American biology. Not until the mid 1950s, however, did the technique start to be generally known and employed in the U.S., where it became increasingly popular in psychological and educational research.

ANOVA was not for an experimenter averse to calculations. Simple and particularly complex ANOVA demand more number crunching than the chi-square tests, z-tests, or t-tests, but not usually as much as Pearson's multiple and partial correlation coefficients. As an aside, the agricultural origin of the analysis of variance may be seen in the name split-plot given to one ANOVA experimental design, plot referring to a piece of land. I have covered ANOVA in detail because it is an exceedingly important and popular tool for discovering and describing multivariate causal relationships.

The last thing to be said about Fisher is he did much to clarify and promote the concept of the statistical significance of differences. Fisher saw (statistically) significant differences as differences which *signify*, or mean, that sample information (a statistic) and population information (a parameter) are not essentially the same or, as he put it, are significantly different. He indicated that a significant difference is caused by a systematic influence exerted on a statistic by something systematically done to things in a sample during the course of an experiment. Fisher's interest in significance appears to have been sparked by what English economist Francis Edgeworth commenced advocating in the 1880s: look for noteworthy/significant changes, not merely changes.

When data on an interval/ratio characteristic are normally distributed, their dispersion, measured as the standard deviation, is interpreted thusly. A calculated standard deviation, say five, is the deviation from the mean of 68% of the data. It, five, is said to be one standard deviation. Doubling and tripling it, we get two standard deviations (ten, or two times five) and three standard deviations (fifteen, or three times five). Inasmuch as the data are distributed normally and hence constitute a normal distribution, we automatically know from the properties of the normal distribution that one, two, and three standard deviations in data respectively encompass 68%, 95%, and 99.7% of all data in a sample. Let us turn from this distribution of data to the distribution of some statistic. We can speak of one, two, and three standard errors of this statistic and thus of one, two, or three standard deviations of its sampling distribution. Also, we can speak of one, two, or three standard errors of said statistic as respectively spanning 68%, 95%, and 99.7% of all instances of it that could be calculated as a result of obtaining from a population all possible random samples of the same size. However, we can say this only when working with certain statistics, mostly sample means and proportions.

The above percentages are related to probabilities. Specifically, the percentages 68%, 95%, and 99.7 % correspond to the probabilities 0.68, 0.95, and 0.997. A *probability* asserts that something will occur while a *percentage* asserts something *did occur.* Now statisticians view significance as a probability and risk as a percentage corresponding to a probability. Both significance and risk exist in degrees. Thus, statisticians talk about levels of significance and levels of risk. Any level of significance can be adopted in a study designed to find the significance of the difference between statistics, although the customary level adopted is either 0.05 or 0.01. The significance level picked will mirror and stem from the risk level, traditionally 5% or 1%, chosen by the person that will do the study. Once a level of significance is adopted, it will be the basis for judging whether the statistic calculated from data collected is vs isn't significant or, in other words, is vs isn't due to systematic variation. This judgment entails referring the statistics to a sampling distribution or a probability distribution, which offer probabilities for use as significance levels.*

Offhand, it would appear significance testing covers all that's relevant to determining significance. What more could be needed or wanted? In 1933, Jerzy Neyman and Egon Pearson suggested an improvement in Fisher's significance testing approach that became known as the hypothesis testing approach. Their approach started to attract a following in the 1950s. During the early 1960s it largely replaced his approach. The result is that inferential techniques for determining significance, which in the 1940s began being termed significance tests, commenced during the 1960s being also referred to as hypothesis tests. How do the significance testing and hypothesis testing approaches differ?

Testing the significance of a difference (either between a statistic and a standard or between two or more statistics) assumes one of four outcomes will take place:

1. deciding the difference is significant and it is significant,

2. deciding the difference is significant and it is not significant,

3. deciding the difference is not significant and it is not significant, or

4. deciding the difference is not significant and it is significant.

Significance testing takes into account the first and second outcomes. Its significance/ risk level addresses the second outcome and thus being wrong deciding the difference observed is significant.

Significance testing sees the decision to be made as that between two hypotheses about a difference (between a statistic and a standard or between two or more statistics). One hypothesis is a research hypothesis; the other is a null hypothesis. The research hypothesis, also called the alternative hypothesis (since it is the alternative to the null hypothesis), states there is a significant difference. Depending upon the purpose of a study, the difference it hypothesizes will be non- directional (i.e., embrace all differences greater than and less than such-and-such size difference) or directional (i.e., embrace all differences greater than or less than such-and-such size difference). A research hypothesis is a composite hypothesis, indicating it addresses a whole spectrum of differences. The null hypothesis states there is no significant difference. It is a simple hypothesis because it includes just one size of difference; namely, zero difference. Only simple and thus null hypotheses can be tested!

The decision made is based upon the results of testing a null hypothesis. If testing the null hypothesis results in it being rejected, then the research hypothesis is accepted. If testing a null hypothesis results in it being retained, then the research hypothesis is treated as being unsupported. Now testing a null hypothesis is achieved by employing a significance test to determine the significance vs insignificance of a difference. If the difference turns out significant, then the null hypothesis is rejected. If it ends up being not significant, then the null hypothesis is retained. Notice that it is common practice to say that the null hypothesis is retained, not accepted, and that the research hypothesis is unsupported, not rejected.

Neyman and Pearson started where Fisher left off. They took into account all four outcomes possible in a situation and then proceeded to explicitly view the situation as a decision-making problem wherein the researcher decides between two hypotheses, the null hypothesis and the research hypothesis. By their hypothesis testing approach acknowledging the third and fourth outcomes listed on page 32, it acknowledges the second type of mistake, or error, a researcher can make. It even tells us how to control and measure this type of error. The first type of error is addressed in significance testing. It is the second outcome: deciding a difference is significant when it is not significant, which leads to rejecting a true null hypothesis and thus accepting a false research hypothesis. The second type of error, unaddressed in significance testing, is the fourth outcome: deciding a difference is not significant when it is significant, which leads to retaining a false null hypothesis and thus regarding a true research hypothesis as unsupported. These two kinds of errors are respectively dubbed a Type I error and a Type II error.

The same decision is made in hypothesis testing as is made in significance testing. It is to accept the research hypothesis vs regard it unsupported by rejecting vs retaining the null hypothesis, in light of deciding a difference is vs isn't significant. Hypothesis testing takes into consideration the Type I error, adds to it the Type II error, and asks a researcher to do his best to control the Type II error.

A seesaw relationship exists between Type I and Type II errors. If all in a situation were to stay constant except for the probabilities of Type I and Type II errors and if the Type I error probability (termed alpha, the significance level adopted) is decreased (e.g., from 0.10 to 0.01), then we find the Type II error probability (termed beta) will increase (e.g., from 0.10 to 0.30). One way to get a low alpha without an unacceptably high beta is to increase the number of things in the sample(s) studied - to increase sample size - by about fifty percent, say from forty to sixty things per sample. Another way is to adopt a research hypothesis whose difference is directional instead of non-directional, as long as this can be sensibly done. That would give us the alpha we want (e.g., 0.05) and a lower beta. It does so by enabling us to legitimately adopt for our criterion an alpha twice as high (i.e., 0.10). Still another way is to choose that significance test, among two or more applicable to the situation considered, with the most power. A test's power is its ability to keep beta small and is defined as one minus beta (e.g., $1.00 - 0.20 = 0.80$).

This might be a good time to say the criterion mentioned on pages 16 and 22 is ordinarily termed the critical value in determinations of significance, due to its critical role. A critical value is that value, out of all the many values embodying a sampling distribution (e.g., the chi-square, t, or F distribution) or a probability distribution acting as a sampling distribution (e.g., the normal distribution), to which we refer a test statistic calculated from sample data. It is that value dictated by the significance level underlying the risk level we adopt. And it is our basis for deciding whether this test statistic is vs isn't significant and thus whether we ought to reject vs retain our null hypothesis and ultimately accept our research hypothesis vs deem it unsupported. An example of a critical value is a 'z' value of 1.96.

Of the various mathematical tables a person may consult are those containing the critical values associated with sampling distributions and aptly termed tables of critical values. The critical values in these tables are called tabled values since they are in the body of a table. When the normal probability distribution acts as a sampling distribution the critical value sought (a z value) is listed along the left side and top of its table and not in the body, its body showing all probabilities (e.g., 0.475) associated with all z values (e.g., 1.96). Tables of critical values are not utilized as much nowadays because statistical software packages generate whatever critical values are appropriate to evaluate the test statistics they calculate from the sample data fed them.

The decision that a difference is vs is not significant and hence is vs is not caused by systematic variation follows from comparing the magnitudes of a test statistic (e.g., z or t) and a critical value (i.e., z or t). Test statistics and critical values may be positive numbers or negative numbers. Positive numbers are implicitly preceded by a plus sign and negative numbers are explicitly preceded by a minus sign. Whether numbers are positive or negative depends on the sampling distribution involved and on the difference in a research hypothesis being considered non-directional vs directional. Some sampling distributions, like chi-square and F, have positive numbers. Others, like t and the normal distribution's z, have positive numbers and negative numbers.

If the distribution employed has positive numbers, then the research hypothesis must be a non-directional difference. The test of a null hypothesis using such a distribution is known as a one-tailed test/one-sided test: it tells us to reject a null hypothesis when a test statistic is greater than a critical value. But if the distribution has positive and negative numbers then the research hypothesis can be a non-directional or a directional difference. The test of a null hypothesis with this distribution is called a two-tailed test/two-sided test when the research hypothesis is a non-directional difference and a one-tailed test when it is a directional difference. A two-tailed test tells us to reject a null hypothesis if a positive test statistic is greater than a positive critical value or if a negative test statistic is less than a negative critical value. A one-tailed test says to reject a null hypothesis if, based on the direction of the difference, a positive test statistic is greater than a positive critical value or a negative test statistic is less than a negative critical value.

The chain of events and line of reasoning in determining the significance of any difference can be outlined thusly. A test statistic incorporating the difference whose significance is to be determined is compared to a critical value. The comparison leads to the decision that the difference is/is not significant. Said decision leads to the decision that the null hypothesis is not/is true and to the action of rejecting/retaining it. And this decision ends with the decision that the research hypothesis is/is not true and to the action of accepting it/deeming it unsupported.

We will finish our discussion on significance testing and hypothesis testing with a couple of comments. First, a statistic (e.g., the mean) is not compatible with a sampling distribution (e.g., the t distribution) and therefore cannot have its significance determined by being referred to a sampling distribution. That is why a test statistic (e.g., the t-test statistic) is necessary. For test statistics are compatible with sampling distributions. This allows them to serve as the medium by which statistics communicate, so to speak, with critical values. Yet test statistics (e.g., a calculated t) do not correspond perfectly to the critical values (e.g., a critical t) in the sampling distribution (e.g., the t distribution) to which they are referred. The reason is they are calculated differently. Whereas a test statistic is calculated from sample data, a critical value is calculated using the equation that defines a sampling distribution. Nevertheless, the similarity of a test statistic and a critical value is close enough, as long as all assumptions of the significance test are satisfied. Second, the inferential techniques utilized to determine significance can with equal validity be called significance tests and hypothesis tests: the significance tested by a significance test is that of the statistic (e.g., a sample correlation) associated with the parameter (i.e., a population correlation) stated in the null hypothesis which is tested by a hypothesis test.

The last thing covered in this chapter are the many statistical techniques frequently referred to as nonparametric and occasionally called distribution-free. Nonparametric and distribution-free signify these techniques make fewer assumptions than others about the parameters (e.g., population variance) or the shape (e.g., normal) of the distribution of states of a population characteristic on which data are to be collected. A researcher is less apt to run into problems with their assumptions being honored. Most nonparametric techniques were invented between 1935 and 1955 in response to a mounting need for techniques to process data on nominal and ordinal characteristics, and on interval/ratio characteristics when the assumptions made by existing techniques (e.g., the Pearson product-moment correlation coefficient, z-tests, t-tests, and F-test) are not upheld in a situation. Many were American innovations. A lot of the impetus behind developing them was the stream of data on ordinal characteristics that in about 1900 started to pour out of psychological research.

Nearly all nonparametric techniques are inferential. Most of them are significance/ hypothesis tests. The earliest were two significance tests Karl Pearson devised in 1900, his chi-square goodness of fit and independence tests (page 23), and a descriptive technique created by Charles Spearman in 1904, his rank-order correlation coefficient. A thirty-year gap followed, after which a large number were invented. The better known ones are the: Fisher exact probability test (1934), Friedman test (1937), runs test (1939), Kolmogorov-Smirnov goodness of fit test (1941), Wilcoxon rank-sum test (1945), sign test (1946), Cramér coefficient/statistic (1946), Mann-Whitney U test (1947), Wilcoxon signed ranks test (1948), median test (1950), Kruskal-Wallis H test (1952), Goodman and Kruskal gamma (1954). All but the Cramér coefficient and the Goodman and Kruskal gamma were significance tests.

Once the label nonparametric was pinned to the above techniques, about 1950, there came the realization that the opposite of a nonparametric technique must be a parametric technique, as exemplified by Pearson's correlation coefficients, the t-tests, the z-tests, and the F-test. A very readable book, Nonparametric Statistics, written by experimental psychologist Sidney Siegel was published in 1956 and did much to stimulate making use of nonparametric techniques in psychological research and to show how they differ from parametric techniques. In about 1960, two factions began taking shape, proponents of and opponents to nonparametric techniques (especially those that are significance tests). Probably the staunchest defense of nonparametric techniques was launched in a more technical book by another experimental psychologist, James Bradley, published in 1968 and entitled Distribution-free Statistical Tests. The commotion over parametric vs nonparametric techniques subsided during the mid 1970s as each was seen to have a place in data analysis.

Parametric techniques assume their data come from observing states manifested by interval/ratio characteristics. Recall from page 17 that interval characteristics have states which are quantities we can distinguish between by saying one is less than or greater than another by such-and-such. A ratio characteristic is an interval characteristic which has a complete absence of quantity, symbolized by zero. Data on interval/ratio characteristics are typically measurements. Nonparametric techniques assume their data come from observing the states of either nominal characteristics or ordinal/interval/ratio characteristics. A nominal characteristic has states which are categories. And an ordinal characteristic has states which are quantities we can distinguish between only by saying one is less than or greater than another.

Also parametric techniques and those nonparametric techniques applied to ordinal/interval/ratio characteristics assume that their data reflect quantities manifested by continuous, as opposed to discrete, characteristics and therefore can, in theory, be infinitely subdivided, despite our inability in practice to discriminate between very fine gradations in their quantity. An instance of a continuous characteristic is weight. We can think of 50, 50.6, 50.64, 50.644, 50.6447, etc. pounds even though the resolving power of a scale may not exceed one decimal place (i.e., cannot go more than one number to the right of the decimal point). The reason for saying the above techniques assume characteristics are continuous is that they compare their test statistics to critical values in continuous sampling distributions/ probability distributions.

Probability theory classifies probability distributions into continuous distributions and discrete, or discontinuous, distributions. The normal probability distribution and the chi-square, t, and F sampling distributions are continuous while the binomial distribution is discrete. The continuousness of quantities processed by a technique is what is meant in statistics by the term continuity. Sometimes we hear statisticians speak of correcting for continuity or, equivalently, using a correction for continuity. This refers to making categories, which by definition are discrete, and discrete quantities, which are quantities treated as being categories, more compatible with techniques (e.g., the chi-square tests) that refer their calculations to continuous distributions (e.g., the chi-square distribution). Related to correcting for continuity is correcting for ties, or a correction for ties. This refers to making any identical quantities - any ties - spotted among data collected, which can happen with quantities that are ranks, more compatible with these techniques. If, as is almost always the case, an inferential technique assumes characteristics are continuous and if these characteristics are actually discrete, then its inferences regarding them will be less accurate and thus misleading unless they have been corrected for ties.

A feel for many of the better known nonparametric techniques can be gleaned from looking at the kinds of characteristics and types of statistical information they address. Three techniques deal with nominal characteristics. The chi-square goodness of fit and independence tests are significance tests whose chi-square test statistics are calculated utilizing frequencies generated from data. Cramér's statistic is a measure of correlation which is calculated making use of the test statistic calculated for the chi-square test of independence. Various nonparametric techniques deal with ordinal characteristics and may be applicable to data on interval/ratio characteristics when the assumptions made by parametric techniques are not upheld. Goodman and Kruskal's gamma is a measure of correlation calculated with frequencies compiled from data; the sign test is a significance test which also relies on frequencies. Most other nonparametric techniques dealing with ordinal characteristics base their calculations on ranks assigned data (see '6' on page 19). One is the Spearman rank-order correlation coefficient. The rest are significance tests: Wilcoxon's tests, the Mann-Whitney U test, the Kruskal-Wallis H test, and Friedman's test. Some nonparametric significance tests, when performed in connection with large samples (page 26), calculate 'z-test statistics' that are compared to 'critical values of z' appearing in the table for the normal distribution.

Until about 1960, it was generally agreed two assumptions made by two parametric significance tests that started to become popular during the early 1950s must be satisfied. The two assumptions are normality and homogeneity of variance. Normality asserts that data for calculating the statistic(s) used by the test in question are quantities displayed by an interval/ratio characteristic that is distributed in a normal fashion in the population(s) of things bearing this characteristic. Homogeneity of variance asserts that the population variances associated with the population characteristic on which data are collected are the same or, put another way, that the two or more pertinent population variances are equal. The two parametric significance tests are the t-test and F-test. Since 1975, it has been generally agreed that bias due to lack of normality is essentially offset by using samples/groups having at least fifteen things in them and that bias due to lack of variance homogeneity is prevented by using samples/groups of the same size.

Now between 1960 and 1970 a more relaxed attitude sprouted toward meeting the above two assumptions. By 1965, there was a feeling, though not a consensus, that the normality and homogeneity of variance assumptions of the t-test and F-test are largely unimportant. Both tests were touted as robust. Robust meant a strong tendency for no difference to arise between adopted vs actual probabilities of committing Type I errors and Type II errors when a specific condition (e.g., normality) that a specific parametric significance test (e.g., the t-test) assumes must be upheld is not upheld in a situation to which it is applied. If no difference occurs between the adopted, also known as the nominal, and the actual error probabilities when a test assumption is violated, then the test is said to be robust in regard to that assumption.

During the early and mid 1960s, James Bradley did extensive research which confirmed the original belief in the importance of the above two assumptions. An excerpt from his book will show readers that statistics is not devoid of its passionate moments. In speaking of the myth of robustness Bradley (1968, p 25) says:

"It is presumably attributable to a none-too-careful reading of robustness studies by statistical practitioners and to an incautious summarization of results by some of their authors and by the authors of statistical textbooks. It often takes the form of a statement that 'the test is robust against the assumption,' or, worse, that 'the test is robust.' Such a statement represents pure semantic chaos. There is no commonly accepted definition of what constitutes robustness, no agreed-upon criterion which distinguishes between a condition of robustness and one of nonrobustness. Nor does the statement specify the extent of the violation against which the test is alleged to be robust. But the 'amount of robustness' tends to depend (among many other things – see below) upon the 'amount of violation'. Thus the only relevant variable mentioned in the statement is left unquantified.

"The most insidious thing about the Myth of Robustness, however, is that the 'degree' of a test's robustness against violation of a given assumption is strongly dependent upon factors which are not involved in the statement of a test's assumptions, which are often not required in a complete description of the assumption's violation, and which are not mentioned in the usual allegation of robustness, as quoted above. These factors cause no distortion of Type I or Type II errors when all assumptions are met, but greatly influence the distortion occurring under a given violation of assumptions- i.e., the factors interact with whatever violation occurs. Examples of such factors are the following:-----"

Bradley is advocating here for employing nonparametric significance tests in situations where before around 1960 parametric significance tests wouldn't have been used due to their normality or homogeneity of variance assumptions not being met. In truth, neither assumption *usually* needs to be satisfied perfectly. With few exceptions, the major one being when a directional research hypothesis is adopted, approximately normal distributions and roughly equal variances are sufficient. I take approximately and roughly to mean no less than 90% satisfied.

CHAPTER 4

SELECTIVE ELABORATIONS

A lot of has been covered in the last three chapters. If you have understood them fairly well, then you already know more than most people do about statistics. For you know more than a little about the history of statistical thinking, about what statistics tries to accomplish, and about how statistics and probability theory dovetail. To this may be added your being more knowledgeable of the eight common types of statistical information, of samples versus populations, of worthwhile kinds of samples, and of concepts and techniques underlying inferential statistics. No longer are you a stranger to statistical terminology: statistic, parameter, frequency distribution, dispersion, error, correlation, confidence interval, extraneous variable, significance test, significance level, risk level, etc. In this chapter are elaborated certain things previously discussed and certain new things, things you should now be better able to comprehend. The chapter puts frosting on the cake baked in chapters 1, 2, and 3.

Revisiting Randomness

We've seen that statistics is very interested in what in everyday language goes by the name chance and what in mathematics and science goes by the name randomness, be it random samples (page 13), independent observations (page 26), or randomization/random assignment (pages 28, 29, and 30). Interest in randomness, or chance, is interest in random variables. Random variable is a term employed in probability theory and thus in inferential statistics. A random variable is a variable - a characteristic - whose states are manifested/displayed/exhibited at random by things in the population sampled, the population from which a random sample is created. What is meant by random?

One could say random is chance. Accordingly, the random sampling of things in a population or the random occurrence of events is their chance sampling or occurrence. But this says no more than random and chance are synonyms. It's a tautology (circular definition). A true definition is: random/chance is the effect on the things to be sampled or on the events taking place of many unknown and independently acting causes. Now a thing in a sample possesses various characteristics, each existing in one out of two or more states at any moment. And an event is the occurrence of a state of a characteristic. If things in a sample are selected at random or if events occur randomly, then all characteristics of things in the sample or all characteristics of these events necessarily become random variables. For a characteristic rides, so to speak, piggyback on the thing or event possessing it. Whatever happens to the thing/event, happens to its characteristics! This is how a characteristic is transformed into a random variable.

Inferential techniques assume samples and groups created from samples are random in order to assure that data they process are from characteristics which are random variables. The reason they assume this is so they can validly refer their test statistics to the critical values in sampling distributions and probability distributions acting as sampling distributions. Critical values are states of a random variable. Hence characteristics of things/events are made into random variables by means of random sampling and randomization (random assignment) in order to uphold the assumption that a variable is random, an assumption made by all sampling distributions/probability distributions.

Usually it is easy to accurately create two or more random groups from a sample. A mathematical table called a random numbers table is helpful in doing this. However, random groups are typically created by drawing well-shuffled slips of paper from a box or a can. Each slip bears a number identifying a thing in the sample and the box/can is shaken vigorously between draws. Usually it is not easy to accurately create a random sample from a population. If the population is finite as opposed to infinite in size, then its things can all, at least in theory, be identified and listed in a sampling frame (page 14) from which the sample is drawn with the aid of a random numbers table or slips of paper. The process is tricky and requires some expertise. If the population is infinite in size, then all things in it cannot be identified and put on a list. This leads to a way of creating a sample which frequently takes on a 'by gosh, by golly' character. When a researcher is unsure her sample is random, she can conduct the runs significance test (page 36). It looks at the sequence of states of a characteristic of the things picked to be in the sample and indicates whether this sequence is random vs systematic.

Finally, there is a subtle, though important, distinction between random samples and simple random samples (page 14). A random sample is a sample drawn in such a way that each thing in a population chosen to be in the sample has no effect on selecting any other thing in the population to be in the sample. This honors the assumption of all inferential techniques that a sample is independent (page 26). A simple random sample is a random sample which, in addition, assumes that all conceivable samples of the same size have the same probability of becoming the sample picked. And a stratified random sample and a cluster sample are two or more simple random samples that function as the strata of a stratified random sample and the clusters of a cluster sample. Occasionally a systematic sample with a random start or a stratified systematic sample with a random start (page 14) conforms to assumptions made by significance tests geared to simple random samples.

Seeking Significance

Remember that the significance sought with significance tests is always a departure from random/unsystematic/chance variation. It has nothing to do with importance, the typical synonym for significance, or with usefulness. Remember, too, that a researcher is not an indifferent participant in his research. He has a stake in its results and in what they imply for the research hypothesis whose fate is tied to that of the null hypothesis he tests. Indeed, a researcher's self-image and financial well-being largely rest upon what happens to the null hypothesis and, thereby, his pet hypothesis. Publish or perish is short for: either publish research findings on topics of interest to authority figures in your line of work, or perish (i.e., look for another livelihood). It's an expression as germane today as it was when coined around 1960. Productivity and job security go hand-in-hand in all endeavors.

Seeking significance is a balancing act. The level of significance adopted is usually 0.05 or 0.01. Why? Two reasons. First, they are the levels mostly adopted, 0.05 being the level Fisher ordinarily employed. Second, levels lower than 0.01, say 0.001, require larger samples and therefore boost the cost of research while higher levels than 0.05, say 0.10, lead to studies done by a researcher not being taken seriously by other researchers (because as significance level increases, the chances of rejecting a true null hypothesis increase and thus increase the chances of accepting a false research hypothesis). Now in exploratory research, which studies little known topics of little known value, it is acceptable to choose a 0.10 significance level in order to keep within the meager budget that frequently stifles such research. But a significance level higher than this is not acceptable. For the outlay of time, energy, and money in designing and doing an exploratory study is less likely to be rewarded, since the study will be less apt to obtain the quality of information a researcher wants and will be ridiculed by other researchers.

We said on page 33 that a second way to get a low alpha (i.e., the significance level adopted) is to use a directional instead of non-directional research hypothesis. This will cut a study's cost by reducing the size of its sample(s). However, it can be done only if a directional research hypothesis makes sense. Now a quandary sometimes faced with directional research hypotheses is what to do when the null hypothesis is retained yet a look at the data suggests the directional research hypothesis is probably true. How can this be? What happens is the directional research hypothesis formulated while designing a study states one direction (e.g., greater than) yet the data collected as the study is performed go in the opposite direction (i.e., lower than). It might be thought all right to modify the research hypothesis, making it conform to the data. But this is considered unethical. So is processing data with a significance test and reprocessing the same data with another significance test, hoping the second test rejects the null hypothesis that the first test failed to reject.

Measures of Average and Dispersion

A rule of thumb in choosing a measure of average or dispersion is to pick one that uses all data collected on a characteristic of interest and preserves the nature - nominal, ordinal, interval, ratio - of this characteristic. Generally speaking, it is best to use the arithmetic mean as the measure of average for data on interval and ratio characteristics (page 18), the median as the measure for data on ordinal characteristics, and the mode as the measure with nominal/categorical characteristics. The (arithmetic) mean is the sum of all quantities in a group, divided by the number of quantities in the group; the median is that quantity in a group's arrayed quantities below which 50% of the group's quantities fall; and the mode is that category in a group having the largest frequency.

There are important exceptions to the above generalization about the mean. First, the median rather than the mean should be employed with interval/ratio data distributed in a skewed (lopsided) fashion. Second, in settings where it is desired to find the mean of two or more means said mean ought to be a weighted mean when the other means are from samples/groups of different sizes. If, as often happens, a person coming across two or more means doesn't know the sample/group sizes which entered into their calculation, then it would be unwise for him to add up, say, three such means and divide their sum by three to get the mean of these means, called the grand mean. Third, there is no measure of average that is meaningful and hence useful when data come from a frequency distribution having more than one hump (i.e., a bimodal or a multimodal distribution) or no hump at all (e.g., a U-shape distribution or a rectangular distribution, also referred to as a uniform distribution).

The mid-range (i.e., the sum of the smallest quantity and the largest quantity in the data collected, divided by two) is an alternative to the mean that is occasionally plotted on control charts employed for monitoring quality. Harmonic and geometric means are used to specify the average of the rate of change of a ratio characteristic in a time series (page 22). There are two sorts of time series, stationary and nonstationary. While the rate of change of a ratio characteristic (e.g., speed) in a stationary time series does not exhibit systematic increases or decreases with the passage of time, the rate change of a ratio characteristic in a nonstationary time series does systematically increase or decrease over time. The harmonic mean is applicable to a stationary time series (assuming that no data in the series are zeros); the geometric mean is suitable to a nonstationary time series (assuming all data are positive numbers). If the data collected honor their assumptions, then the harmonic and geometric means are more accurate than and thus preferable to the mean. Note that a nonstationary time series is commonly called a growth function when its quantities steadily increase as time passes and a decay function when they steadily decrease. As an aside, I don't know of any inferential techniques that produce confidence interval estimates or determine significance of differences which cater to the measures of average mentioned in this paragraph.

As for measures of dispersion, the standard deviation and the variance are used for data from interval/ratio characteristics having approximately normal distributions. The standard deviation is employed as a descriptive measure, because it is expressed in the same units of measurement as are the data collected, and as a component of inferential techniques, where it is utilized to calculate standard errors. The variance, square of the standard deviation, is the basis for the F-test integral to the analysis of variance (page 28). Now the standard deviation and variance give a poor impression of dispersion in distributions that are not approximately normal. The quartile deviation, or semi-interquartile range, is used with data on ordinal characteristics. Other measures are not used enough to warrant discussing.

Dichotomies

Some characteristics are termed dichotomies. Dichotomies are characteristics that either are known to manifest two states (natural dichotomies) or are *imagined* to manifest two states (artificial dichotomies). A natural dichotomy is a nominal/categorical characteristic (page 16) while an artificial dichotomy is a quantitative (ordinal, interval, or ratio) characteristic. Characteristics treated as dichotomies, especially artificial dichotomies, usually have more than just two states (i.e., categories or quantities). The characteristic known as gender (sex) is treated as a natural dichotomy, whose categories are male and female. Our treating gender this way rests on what we know about gender. It may rest more on what is imagined than on what is known. The characteristic termed intelligence is normally considered an ordinal characteristic exhibiting many quantities. It becomes an artificial dichotomy when treated as displaying two quantities, say below average and above average intelligence. Hardness is an ordinal characteristic manifesting at least ten quantities, the ten in the ten-point Mohs scale of mineral hardness devised in 1812 by the German mineralogist Friedrich Mohs. Yet hardness is often artificially dichotomized by acknowledging only two quantities, hard and soft. Lastly consider vehicle mileage. It is a ratio characteristic having innumerable quantities. Frequently it is desirable to compress all vehicle mileages into merely two, low mileage and high mileage.

Be careful with dichotomies! Two precautions are important. First, sometimes a generally accepted natural dichotomy may not in fact reflect nature but in truth mirror our ignorance of nature. Which may be the case with the nominal characteristic gender. Of course, this is more a concern of research than of statistics. Yet statistics does not get off the hook if it is knowingly employed to legitimize and perpetuate ignorance. Statistics can be a disservice. Whether it is or is not rests upon how its information is applied to the things we wish to know about. It is good for us to question every once in a while a long-standing natural dichotomy in order to be sure we still feel it is valid.

Second, in spite of the frequent desirability of employing artificial dichotomies we should realize that doing so runs contrary to a tradition in statistics and research. This is the habit of collecting and processing data in ways which preserve the nature - nominal, ordinal, interval, or ratio - of a characteristic. As said on page 17, interval characteristics are mostly conveniences in dealing with data from certain ratio characteristics, such as temperature. Now understating the nature of a ratio characteristic by treating it as an interval characteristic is common and is a commonly accepted exception to the tradition. However, understating the nature of an ordinal or interval/ratio characteristic by treating it as an artificial dichotomy is a greater understatement and consequently ought to be done with caution. The first thing to do is to determine what will be accomplished and what will be obscured by dichotomizing a particular quantitative characteristic (e.g., mileage). If after identifying and mulling over pros and cons it is decided to dichotomize, then the next thing to do is to decide on how best to conceptualize and label the quantities. A practice since the 1970s is to label the two states of a dichotomy, be it natural or artificial, in the following way: male vs non-male (instead of male vs female) and low mileage vs not low mileage (rather than low mileage vs high mileage). I think this practice reveals the shortcomings of dichotomization.

More about Correlation

We talked about correlation and correlation vs causation on pages 19 and 20 and about simple, partial, and multiple correlation on page 24. Five more things will be discussed here. First, the numbers produced by measures of correlation - by correlation coefficients - are not to be thought of as probabilities or proportions/relative frequencies. The correlations 0.32, 0.51, 0.67, 0.84, etc. generated using, say, the Pearson product moment correlation coefficient are neither probabilities nor proportions therefore, even though they may look like them because they range from 0.00 through 1.00. Second, all measures of correlation produce positive numbers, or numbers implicitly preceded by plus sign (e.g., 0.84). Most measures of simple correlation where both characteristics are quantitative produce negative numbers too, meaning numbers explicitly preceded by a minus sign (e.g., -0.84). If a coefficient can produce positive or negative numbers, then its positive numbers denote direct relationships (i.e., relationships where increases in the quantities exhibited by one characteristic coincide with increases in the quantities displayed by the other characteristic) and its negative numbers indicate inverse relationships (i.e., relationships where increases in the quantities of one characteristic coincide with decreases in those of the other). Depending on whether no sign or a minus sign is in front of them, the correlations generated by such coefficients are termed positive correlations and negative correlations respectively.

Third, there are differences among correlation coefficients in how they crank out correlations and in the nature of the data they process, which is traceable to the nature of the characteristics they address. Consequently, it is imprudent to think a correlation of 0.75 generated by four measures of correlation - Pearson's product-moment correlation coefficient, the point-biserial correlation coefficient, the correlation ratio (eta), and the Cramér coefficient - is the same strength of relationship. But these four coefficients are enough alike that the same number generated by each will reflect at least very roughly the same strength (i.e., a ballpark figure of between 0.65 and 0.85).*Fourth, the statistical significance of, not the size of, a correlation is what counts! The reason is that a sample correlation of 0.75 does not necessarily stand a better chance than one of 0.50 of being found significant, although usually it does. For while 0.75 is a high correlation which implies a strong relationship, it refers to a sample relationship and not to the population relationship hypothesized to be yielding the sample relationship. Note that a significant sample correlation of 0.75 does not mean the population correlation is 0.75. However, a confidence interval (page 27) erected for this population correlation utilizing this sample correlation and having confidence limits from 0.72 to 0.78 will quickly show these two correlations are essentially the same.

Fifth, a correlation may be branded spurious or spuriously high. Spurious means false. Hence spurious and spuriously high are warnings a person utters to alert other people to her thinking the correlation so branded is suspect and ought to not be taken at face value by them. Naturally this is one person's opinion. It may be right, or it could be wrong. Spurious has been misapplied. A clear misapplication occurs when someone asserts a correlation is spurious upon hearing somebody else say the correlation indicates the relationship in question is causal. This brings to mind the quotation from Bradley on page 38, where he said in regard to a claim made about robustness that "Such a statement represents pure semantic chaos". We know from our earlier discussion that correlation is neither causation nor, by itself, sufficient evidence of causation. Also, we can safely assume statisticians and scientists know this. Thus, labeling a correlation spurious because it is wrongly construed to indicate the presence of a causal relationship is senseless. For what's spurious is not the correlation itself but interpreting it to signify the existence of a causal relationship.

It seems more informative to talk about three degrees of appropriateness in using the concept correlation and in using correlation coefficients than to characterize their usage as valid or spurious. These degrees of appropriateness are: inappropriate, questionable, appropriate. We would then say using the concept or the coefficients as the sole basis for deeming a relationship causal vs noncausal is inappropriate. We would say that it is inappropriate to view numbers produced by correlation coefficients as being proportions or probabilities. We would say that comparing the correlations generated by different correlation coefficients is questionable: if a person does this, then he ought to do it with caution and tell people the name of the coefficient producing each correlation compared. Finally, we'd say it is questionable to calculate a simple correlation when knowing or believing that one or more characteristics lying outside the relationship whose strength is sought are extraneous variables whose unwanted influence will affect the size of any simple correlation calculated, making that correlation either spuriously high (overstating it) or spuriously low (understating it). A partial correlation is needed in such cases. If no partial correlation coefficient is suitable, then it would be better to calculate no simple correlation than to calculate a dubious one.

Proportions and Percentages Linked to Correlation

Many correlation coefficients are so designed that they endow the correlations they generate with a very useful property. Any one of their correlations, say 0.80, can be squared to make a proportion (i.e., 0.80 x 0.80 = 0.64) and that proportion can then be multiplied by 100 in order to make it into a percentage (i.e., 64%). This percentage is a measure of relatively how much the dispersion in states manifested by one characteristic of a relationship is determined, or explained, by the other characteristic(s). If the percentage (e.g., 64%) is subtracted from 100%, then a second percentage results (i.e., 36%). It signifies relatively how much of the dispersion in one characteristic does not stem from the other characteristic(s) of the relationship and consequently may, yet may not, stem from one or more characteristics lying outside the relationship. Recollect from page 29 that a characteristic/variable outside a relationship which influences the relationship goes by the names extraneous, lurking, and nuisance variable.

The value of these two percentages is they convey a more meaningful impression of the strength of a relationship, by telling us how much of its strength may be the result of one or more extraneous variables. Too small a percent for the first percentage, say less than 50%, and thus too large a percent for the second, more than 50%, ought to trigger some reflecting upon these percentages. Do they reflect no more than just a moderately strong relationship? Or do they imply a relationship that is under the influence of things outside it? If the correlation was simple and if reflection suggests the percentages stem from identifiable extraneous variables, then new data should be collected. These data would be on characteristics of the relationship and on certain characteristics which are strongly felt to be powerful extraneous variables. After new data are collected they can be transformed into either a partial correlation (if the desire is that the bivariate relationship remain a bivariate relationship) or a multiple correlation (if the desire is to make the bivariate relationship into a multivariate relationship).

Correlation coefficients producing correlations from which such percentages can be validly calculated are the Pearson product-moment correlation coefficient, the Pearson product-moment multiple correlation coefficient, the Pearson product-moment partial correlation coefficient, the correlation ratio, the point-biserial correlation coefficient (Hays, 1994, p 336), and the Spearman rank-order correlation coefficient (Mendenhall et al., 1974, p 374). The first percentage and its proportion are called the coefficient of determination with the Pearson product-moment correlation coefficient and the coefficient of multiple determination with the Pearson product-moment multiple correlation coefficient. The second percentage and its proportion are known as the coefficient of nondetermination in both cases. As for the correlation ratio, or eta, the first percentage and its proportion are termed eta squared (the 'e' sounds like a in ate).

Akin to these squared correlation measures is a measure calculated from the t-test statistic and the sample sizes of a t-test conducted on two means whose data come from independent observations (page 26). It is the estimate of omega squared: the proportion of dispersion in quantities of an interval/ratio characteristic explained by the difference between the states of a dichotomous characteristic (Hays, 1994, p 337). It is obtained as follows. First, square the t-test statistic. Second, subtract the squared t-test statistic from one. The difference is the numerator of the formula used to calculate the estimate. Third, subtract one from the sum of the squared t-test statistic and the two sample sizes. Put this difference in the denominator of the formula. Fourth, divide the number in the formula's numerator by the number in the formula's denominator. The quotient is the estimate of omega squared. It is a number that can go from 0.00 (negative quotients are treated as zero) through 1.00 or, multiplied by 100, from 0% through 100%.

Contingency Tables

Research performed in certain social sciences, especially in sociology and political science, is often oriented toward discovering and describing relationships between two, three, or four characteristics which usually are nominal but sometimes are ordinal. It is common for ordinal characteristics in these studies to be treated as nominal characteristics. Hence their quantities are commonly conceived as categories and identified using words (e.g., young, middle aged, old) rather than numbers and words (e.g., 17, 48, 79 years old). Data collected on categories of nominal and ordinal characteristics are transformed into frequencies, or counts. Each frequency is the number of times a particular combination of categories (e.g., male, oriental, and old) manifested by the characteristics studied (i.e., gender, race, and age) was observed in the things studied (i.e., people) and was therefore observed to jointly occur and thus be a joint event. This is why each such frequency is more specifically known as a joint frequency. The number of joint frequencies is equal to the number of categories studied. If a study entails three characteristics respectively displaying two, four, and three categories, then the number of categories and, as a result, the number of joint frequencies compiled will be 2 x 4 x 3 = 24.

After their compilation these, say 24, joint frequencies are placed within the body of a kind of frequency table termed a contingency table. A contingency table is a set of intersecting (crisscrossing) horizontal and vertical lines that form rows and columns which serve to distinguish one characteristic from another as well as one category from another. Intersections of lines produce boxes termed cells. Joint frequencies are appropriately put inside the cells, whereupon joint frequencies are also called cell frequencies. The result is four or more cross-classifications/cross-tabulations/cross-tabs/cross-partitions/cross breaks. Cell frequencies/joint frequencies in each row are added together and their sum is put in a row's right margin; cell frequencies in each column are added up and their sum is placed in a column's bottom margin. A table's various row totals and column totals are generated this way.

Now the number of characteristics and categories depicted by the rows and by the columns of a table are employed to designate the table. A table with one row characteristic having three categories and one column characteristic having five categories is designated a 3 x 5 contingency table. It would have 3x5 = 15 cells and thus 15 cell frequencies. Sometimes a table with one row characteristic and one column characteristic is termed a bivariate frequency table. A table with one row characteristic having two categories, one column characteristic having four categories, and one column characteristic having three categories is a 2 x 4 x 3 contingency table. It would have 24 cells and 24 cell frequencies.

Contingency tables are best known for their use in conjunction with the chi-square test of independence. When so utilized, each cell in a table has a small cell in its top right corner. In the small cell is the expected frequency for a cell as opposed to the cell frequency compiled from data, known as the observed frequency. The chi-square test of independence operates by determining if differences between observed and expected cell frequencies are large enough to indicate a significant difference does vs doesn't exist between them. From this is decided whether a relationship does vs doesn't exist between the characteristics. A chi-square test of independence that addresses a bivariate relationship, like the one implied in the preceding 3x5 contingency table, is what is meant by simple chi-square. And a chi-square test of independence addressing a multivariate relationship, as implied in the preceding 2x4x3 contingency table, is what's meant by complex chi-square. Parenthetically, the chi-square test statistic calculated in the chi square test of independence is occasionally employed to calculate Cramér's statistic, a measure of correlation which is an improved version of the contingency coefficient that Karl Pearson invented.

It should be pointed out that contingency tables are used with other significance tests too and with measures functioning somewhat the way measures of correlation do. These measures generate proportions specifying by how much errors made in predicting states of one nominal characteristic in a bivariate relationship are reduced by knowing states of the other nominal characteristic, a concept which arose about 1960 and goes by the name proportional reduction in errors. Two proportional reduction in error, or PRE, measures are the tau - pronounced tow, as in towel - and the lambda that Goodman and Kruskal devised. Blalock (1979; pp 307-311, p 315) thought tau is superior to both lambda and the Cramér coefficient.

Regression

In the 1920s, Ronald Fisher pioneered the versatile technique called the analysis of variance or ANOVA. Two decades earlier, Karl Pearson pioneered the equally versatile technique called regression analysis or regression. Both techniques are still key ways to discover and describe multivariate relationships between characteristics. Fisher's technique relies on determining the significance of differences between sample variances (via the F-test) so as to determine the significance of differences between sample means and thereby learn whether there exists a population relationship between characteristics. It got its feet wet on bivariate relationships (i.e., simple ANOVA), as did regression (i.e., simple regression). Regression relies on determining the significance of the difference of the slope of a regression line in simple regression or the slopes of a regression surface in multiple regression (via the F-test and/or t-test) so as to learn whether there exists a population relationship between characteristics.

Regression is an extension of correlation. How so? Correlation specifies the strength of a relationship. And the significance test run on a sample correlation tells us whether the sample correlation differs significantly from what the null hypothesis says the population correlation is; namely, that it is zero (indicating no population relationship exists). If the significance test says to reject the null hypothesis and accept the research hypothesis, then we will want to next describe the relationship. Now a relationship can be described verbally (in words) and often mathematically, either graphically (i.e., with a graph) or analytically (i.e., by an equation). Analytical descriptions of relationships are more precise than graphical descriptions of them, which are more precise than verbal descriptions.

Upon discovering the relationship's strength to be enough to consider it exists in the population of interest, we would next try to create what is termed a regression equation in order to describe it. For a bivariate relationship, the regression equation will include in it two study variables (page 29): one dependent and one independent variable. And for a multivariate relationship, the equation will include three or more study variables: one dependent variable and two or more independent variables. The dependent variable will be placed left of the equals sign in the regression equation; the independent variable(s) will be placed to the right of this sign. Regression analyses expect - assume - data processed on every variable/characteristic in a regression equation honor what is known as the least squares criterion that is integral to the method of least squares, which is used to calculate the slope(s) in a regression equation. This expectation is satisfied only if every variable is related to every other variable in a linear fashion (i.e., there is a linear, or straight-line, relationship between every pair of variables). By the way, a slope is the rate at which the dependent variable changes with changes in an independent variable, said rate being constant, or a constant, in any linear relationship between variables.

In addition to the above 'linearity' prerequisite, regression analyses assume three more things. First, the dependent variable and at least one independent variable in a regression equation is an interval/ratio characteristic. Second, quantities of the dependent variable are distributed in an (approximately) normal manner for each state of each independent variable. Third, the variance of the dependent variable is (roughly) the same for all states of an independent variable, although this need not hold across all independent variables. If the assumptions of linearity, normality, or homogeneity of variance are not met, then they can usually be met by transforming data on the dependent variable and/or the independent variable(s) in a certain way (e.g., converting them into square roots, reciprocals, or common logarithms). This can also be done in the ANOVA. Data transformation is a trial-and-error process of looking for not only what will work but what will work without adversely affecting assumptions already satisfied.

Multiple Comparisons

The expression multiple comparison comes out of a research context, principally an experimental research context. It pertains to what, statistically, is done after uncovering a significant overall difference between three or more statistics. Typically, these statistics are sample means and the significant *overall difference* between them is found by using the analysis of variance (see italicized on page 30). Occasionally these statistics are sample rank-sums that are found, by doing the Kruskal-Wallis H test or maybe the Friedman test, to differ significantly as a *whole*.

After ascertaining that the overall difference between three or more statistics is significant it is possible, and advisable, for a researcher to inquire into which of the three or more individual differences comprising this overall difference are vs aren't significant, since one or more may not be significant. Doing this entails using a technique specially designed to determine more than one significant difference at a crack and thus compare multiple differences or, equivalently, make multiple comparisons or contrasts. The word specially here means the techniques considered make their comparisons without allowing the level of risk the researcher adopted, the nominal level predicated on the significance level adopted, to increase as she proceeds from one comparison to the next. Such an inflation in the nominal significance level/risk level would take place were she to perform these comparisons the commonsensical way by doing t-tests after a significant F-test (in an ANOVA), doing Wilcoxon rank-sum tests after a significant Kruskal-Wallis H test, or doing sign tests after a significant Friedman test. The level of significance/risk adopted, say 0.05/5%, before doing the first of, say, four comparisons could skyrocket to an actual significance/risk level of 0.20/20% with the fourth comparison made!

In around 1963 there appeared a set of journal articles, often called the Ryan papers, which summarized and drew conclusions about research, since around 1950, on inflation of alpha (the nominal/adopted significance level) when making multiple comparisons and how to curb it. This research found that bivariate significance tests which specialize in multiple comparisons can be engineered to prevent inflation. Also, it found that precisely how inflation is stopped depends upon whether the multiple comparisons made in a study are planned (i.e., decided on when the study is being designed and hence before any data are collected) vs unplanned/post hoc (i.e., decided on after the study collects data).

A number of multiple comparison significance tests were invented during the 1950s for use in conjunction with the analysis of variance: the Newman-Keuls method (1952), the Scheffé method (1953), Tukey's honestly significant difference/HSD test (1953), Duncan's new multiple range test (1955), the Dunnett test (1955), etc. Most of them employed a modified t-test or a modified t distribution or limited the comparisons made with an ordinary t-test to what's called orthogonal (independent) comparisons. Readers wanting to know more are referred to Glass & Hopkins (1996, pp 444-469) and Roscoe (1975, pp 309-322). Also there is a multiple comparison test which is utilized with the Kruskal-Wallis H test (Siegel & Castellan, 1988, pp 206-216) and another which is used with the Friedman test (Siegel & Castellan, 1988, pp 174-184).

Bayesian Statistics

Bayesian statistics arose in the late 1950s, as did Bayesian decision-making. They embraced an old idea just starting to be refurbished under a new name. Ever since the dawn of mankind we've relied on what has long gone by names like intuition, hunches, gut feelings, etc. Such 'things' are vague and reflect the still mysterious way that we individually process data into information for use in navigating a world and life full of largely unpredictable occurrences. It was the desire to get around this vagueness that inspired the founding of probability theory by two Frenchmen in 1654 (page 7). The theory largely circumvented vagueness by its laws of chance/randomness and with the probabilities based upon them, a probability being a number ranging from 0.00 (it will not occur) through 1.00 (it will occur). Initially, reason was used to create probabilities. Said probabilities are rational (reason-based) probabilities. They were the only probabilities for 200 years. From 1860 to 1910, observing frequencies of events increasingly became another way to create probabilities, a relative frequency (e.g., 0.30) based on fifty or more observations becoming a probability (i.e., 0.30). Advocates of this approach to probability were England's John Venn, America's Charles Peirce, and England's Karl Pearson. Said probabilities are empirical (observation-based) probabilities. By 1915, there were rational probabilities and empirical probabilities.

From 1925 to 1960, people began to increasingly employ reason to better grasp what might be called intuitive prediction. The result was a gradual refurbishing of an old idea, intuitive prediction, and naming it personal (intuition-based) probability. Like rational and empirical probabilities, a personal probability is a number between 0.00 and 1.00. Unlike them, the number in a personal probability signifies an individual's belief or feeling that such-and-such will not occur (0.00) vs will occur (1.00). Personal probability was conceived by the Englishman Frank Ramsey in 1926, pondered and refined over the next 25 years, dignified in 1954 by the American Leonard Savage asserting that it is a foundation stone of statistics, and by the American Robert Schlaifer showing in his 1959 book how personal probabilities can be utilized for solving a variety of manufacturing and business problems. Around 1960, rational and empirical probabilities started to be collectively referred to as objective probabilities while personal probabilities began being also dubbed subjective probabilities. So, by 1960 there were objective probabilities and subjective/personal probabilities.

Steadily from the late 1950s onward subjective probabilities were inserted in a relationship between probabilities called Bayes' theorem which was invented in about 1740 by Thomas Bayes, a Scottish clergyman and mathematician. His theorem evoked little interest until around 1890. That's when it commenced to be used by some and misused by others who viewed it as a tool for making causal inferences about all kinds of things. Flagrant misuse led to Bayes' theorem falling into disrepute in the 1920s. But by 1955, safeguards in applying it legitimately had been identified and implemented, resulting in a renewed and even greater interest in the theorem. About that time, people enthused with subjective probability became just as enthusiastic over Bayes' theorem. For they saw in it a way to integrate a subjective probability about a thing with an objective probability about the thing. Essentially, the theorem revises - upgrades - an existing probability by reversing what is known as a conditional probability and then making an inference about this reversal, a type of inference called Bayesian inference. The importance attached to Bayesian inference by promoters of a subjective probability approach to decision-making led in the 1960s to their approach being termed Bayesian decision-making. Yet while Bayesian decision-making thrived from 1965 onward, Bayesian statistics didn't. Today, Bayesian statistics is occasionally used by a few to largely make confidence interval estimates of population means and proportions (see Miller & Freund, 1985).

Statistical Decision Theory

Paralleling the development of subjective probability was the evolution of decision theory, now typically termed statistical decision theory. Decision theory is a normative theory because it sets forth norms which prescribe - tell - a person what to do or what alternative action to take in a situation. In this respect, decision theory is unlike most theories. Most theories, scientific or nonscientific, are explanatory theories: they explain a relationship between characteristics. A theory prescribing how to make optimal decisions and hence make decisions that are the best possible in light of what somebody knows about a situation is traceable to the brilliant American-Hungarian mathematician John von Neumann. He sketched in 1928 and elaborated in 1944 a normative theory telling a person how to make optimal decisions when competing with another person and thereby being in a conflict situation, meaning a situation where one person's gain or loss influences another person's gain or loss. Such decision-making situations resemble in their competition and conflict the games played by two people or by two teams and the interactions between two companies out to win over the same clientele or two nations after the same resources. This is why his theory is named game theory.

One rule von Neumann regarded useful in competitive situations for deciding what action to take or, as put by game theory, what strategy to adopt is the minimax decision rule, or decision criterion. It would shortly become a decision rule in decision theory too. The minimax rule gets its name from instructing the decision maker to take that action/ adopt that strategy which, according to an analysis of a situation, will always lead to him obtaining the minimum of the maximum undesirable consequences possible in the situation. Decision theory was pieced together in the late 1940s by American-Austrian mathematician Abraham Wald. It addresses situations not marked by competition/conflict. In the late 1950s, the theory began to emphasize the benefits of a decision maker adopting one particular decision rule; namely, the maximizing expected value criterion. Since expected value is a concept of probability theory and, by extension, of statistics, emphasizing it led to decision theory becoming generally known as statistical decision theory. A couple of incidentals are worth noting. First, applying (statistical) decision theory to situations is called decision analysis. Second, during the 1970s and 1980s a few textbooks on statistics, chiefly those discussing the theory's relevance to business and economics, portrayed the field of statistics as decision-making.

CHAPTER 5

PARTING THOUGHTS

In this, the final chapter, are offered insights and tips on using statistics. Learning them will further improve your statistical literacy. We will deal more with inferential statistics than descriptive statistics and more with significance determinations than parameter estimates. In what follows is information you should know if you expect to use statistics. By using statistics, I mean using your knowledge about statistics to understand the ever-increasing statistical information on crime, medical procedures, education issues, consumer safety, immigration, economic cycles, foreign affairs, poverty, climate change, health problems, etc. that you learn from television, newspapers, magazines, books, reports, pamphlets, internet websites, etc. If you want to learn more about statistics, then the next step is to get and study an introductory college textbook on statistics that covers the many fields to which statistics is applied. I find the textbook by Mario Triola (2006) to be very good.

Don't be timid asking for clarification of statistical information someone gives you about something. Statistical information may be vague because a person purveying it is so familiar with it that he or she forgets others may not be. Or its purveyor may intend it to be ambiguous in hopes of leading you to think along lines he wants you to think, in a direction that unbeknownst to you is either not supported or poorly supported by this information. Unscrupulous individuals realize most people are simultaneously impressed with and intimidated by numbers, and so they relish conveying numerical information. Watch out for overly precise data and statistics, whose precision is unjustified and likely intended to deceive.

It is important when doing the string of calculations required to calculate some statistics (e.g., the mean) to not round off your numbers by less than four decimal places - to less than four spaces after the decimal point - until reaching the final calculation. That calculation (e.g., 173.8333) is the statistic (e.g., mean weight in pounds) to be calculated and should be rounded to one place after the decimal point (i.e., 173. 8). However, if this statistic is to be utilized in calculating another statistic (e.g., a standard deviation) then it should not be rounded. There is an exception to the rounding rule. It concerns calculated proportions/relative frequencies and calculated probabilities. Both should be calculated to five decimal places (e.g., 0.36549) and rounded to two decimal places (i.e., 0.37), unless they are going to be employed in subsequent calculations and thus should be left unrounded. Rarely do the data collected contain any negative numbers (e.g., -12). If any data are negative numbers, then your calculator or computer knows how to relate them to one another and to positive numbers. Two recommendations when calculating are: do a set of calculations twice to make sure the final calculation is correct and do not calculate when groggy or in the wrong mood.

Sample size affects statistical inferences. It is more consequential with parameter estimates than significance determinations. For an increase in size of a sample improves the preciseness of a parameter estimate. In the case of (confidence) interval estimates, a relatively large sample yields a relatively small interval within which the parameter estimated is likely to occur. Formulae exist for indicating how large a sample is needed to construct a confidence interval no wider than such-and-such for a confidence level of such-and-such. The higher the confidence level desired the wider and less precise will be the confidence interval created, unless sample size is increased noticeably to prevent this widening. A sample of a few hundred things is commonly encountered with parameter estimates. With significance determinations a sample is vastly smaller, usually numbering fifteen to fifty things. This is as it should be. For too large a sample, say a hundred things, can result in statistical significance (e.g., 0.001) devoid of any practical significance. By this is meant the difference found is not large enough to make a difference in how we think or act. I've said the above things so you know what to do if ever calculating statistics and know how to reflect upon calculations not known to you which underlie statistical information you come across.

A population in the report on a study may not be the population from which the study got its sample(s). Either of two reasons typically account for this. One is mistaken identity: the population sampled seemed, maybe without much careful thought, to be this target population, say A, but was really another population, say B. You might infer the discrepancy from the study's report if it gives sufficient details about how its sample(s) was created. Misidentifying a population can subtly happen when the population sampled is a finite population and the sampling frame (page 14) listing all things in it is out of date. Perhaps the frame grew obsolescent due to the state manifested by the parameter inherent to it, the parameter of interest, slowly changing over the last ten years, unbeknownst to the researcher. Hence, the target population no longer exists because it evolved into the population sampled. Note that a parameter which varies - a population characteristic whose state varies - as time passes is known as a time-varying parameter. Time-varying parameters are the rule, not exception, and the reason for why longitudinal kinds of studies are conducted.

The other reason for a disparity between the sampled and target populations could be the target population is unfeasible to sample and consequently a population assumed to be like it is sampled instead. An example is psychological research done at American colleges for decades in which a group of undergraduate college students is observed so as to learn about a relationship between human psychological characteristics (e.g., between reading ability, verbal aptitude, and achievement motivation). The group studied is a convenience sample (page 14) and not a random sample. What's learned about the convenience sample is generalized to - viewed as being true of - a target population. One problem with this is the sample is not random. Another is that the target population is seldom clearly defined in the research report written. Is it the current population of undergraduate students at the American college sponsoring the research? Or is it the current population of undergraduates at all American colleges? Or is the target population the current population of all Americans 15 to 25 years old? You may not know from the report. But you would suspect the research was not done merely to know the relationship in the group studied.

If data are processed by employing the Spearman rank-order correlation coefficient, Wilcoxon rank-sum test, Mann-Whitney U test, Kruskal-Wallis H test, Wilcoxon signed ranks test, or Friedman test and if a large number of ties occur in the ranks created, then a correction for ties, or ties correction factor, should be used when calculating them. By a tie in ranks, or tied rank, is meant the same rank number, say five, is assigned more than once to data collected in a study. The reason for utilizing a correction for ties is that it offsets the loss in continuity which is caused by ties. A large number of uncorrected tied ranks overstates a Spearman correlation, making it spuriously high. Also a large number of uncorrected ties in ranks will understate the test statistic of, and thereby decrease the chance of getting a significant difference with, the Wilcoxon rank- sum/Mann-Whitney U test (if these ties exist between the two samples studied, as opposed to within them), the Kruskal-Wallis H test, the Wilcoxon signed ranks test, and the Friedman test. Some introductory statistics texts covering the above techniques are a bit skimpy on details about calculating tie correction factors. A detailed discussion on calculating them is found in Siegel and Castellan (1988).

Never lose sight of the fact that statistical techniques have limitations. First, they are limited by the situations to which they can be applied. These restrictions are often stated as assumptions they make about a situation. Inferential techniques make more assumptions - have more restrictions - than descriptive techniques. This is especially true of inferential techniques geared to determining the significance of differences (i.e., significance tests/ hypothesis tests). Nonetheless, the assumptions of descriptive techniques, while rarely called assumptions per se, are important too. The mean should not be utilized as the measure of average for data from an interval/ratio characteristic whose quantities form a skewed (frequency) distribution. In other words, the mean is restricted to, or permissible with, an interval/ratio characteristic whose quantities are configured as a normal distribution. To this can be added that the Pearson product-moment correlation coefficient assumes data it processes are from two interval/ratio characteristics and that a scatter diagram (page 20) shows the characteristics to be linearly related. If the diagram indicates a nonlinear relationship, then the strength of their relationship should be assessed employing the correlation ratio (eta).

Honoring assumptions can be a juggling act. After checking for satisfaction of the assumptions of a descriptive technique, the next thing is to see if assumptions of an inferential technique are met (since usually our interest is in knowing the parameter associated with the statistic a descriptive technique creates). Once a study is done, the data collected may reveal that an assumption of the descriptive technique or the inferential technique is violated. If a data transformation does not solve the problem, then another descriptive technique and/or inferential technique must be found. Now, honoring the assumptions of a significance test can be looked upon this way. The two, three, or more assumptions it makes cover all ways, except one, that it will react to a situation by announcing a significant difference exists. By assuring all its assumptions are met we narrow the cause of the announcement down to one, the statistics being tested. Another thing to be mindful of is that statistical techniques are limited insofar as how much their calculations will tell you about a population. Consider regression equations. What they can say is restricted to observed quantities of the one or more independent variables in them. To generalize to quantities smaller than the smallest quantity observed or larger than the largest observed quantity is to say the relationship holds - is the same - for these unobserved quantities as well, a claim nearly never justifiable. This goes for all research!

Other than his supporting England's eugenics movement, the sole blemish on Karl Pearson's sterling career was him thinking that poor quality data could almost always be made into good quality data through careful application of statistical techniques. This prompts my last comment on the limits of such techniques, which is they are very limited in their ability to salvage flawed data and therefore are basically subject to the principle "garbage in, garbage out". Hence, it is extremely important that the process whereby data will be collected is thought out meticulously before starting to actually collect data. Pitfalls to avoid include not calibrating measuring devices needing periodic calibration, not assessing beforehand the reliability, validity, and thus acceptability of a questionnaire to be utilized in a survey, not training or not supervising the people tasked with collectting data, and not determining beforehand the expertise and reputability of individuals/organizations supplying data they possess and you have requested (for use in a study you plan to conduct).

The last paragraph introduced you to considerations involving methodology, which is all methods that enter into doing research. Statistics is the chief mathematical method for analyzing/processing data. Herein lies the link between statistics and methodology. There are two methodological matters, or matters regarding method, to be aware of when doing a study or reading a report on the findings of a study. One is the occurrence of interactions; the other is the occurrence of confounding. Interactions and confounding affect how the results of a study are interpreted.

Interaction, as used here, is a special relationship between two or more independent variables in an experiment (pages 29 and 30). An interaction exists when the effect on the dependent variable (e.g., reading ability) of one independent variable (e.g., verbal aptitude) is affected by one or more other independent variables (e.g., achievement motivation) or, equivalently, the influence one independent variable exerts on the dependent variable is itself influenced by the influence of the other independent variable(s) on the dependent variable. Whereas the two or more independent variables are said to interact, to be interacting, or to be an interaction, the effect of their interaction on the dependent variable is said to be an interaction effect. Significant interaction effects are important to know because they will alter the interpretation of main effects, a main effect being the effect of one independent variable on the dependent variable. Experimental designs for analysis of variance can reveal the respective influences of each main effect and each interaction effect on a dependent variable.

Confounding is obscuring, hiding, or masking the influence an independent variable exerts upon a dependent variable by letting changes in states of the independent variable coincide with changes in states of another variable, referred to as a confounding variable. The independent variable is said to be confounded with or by this other variable, or to be confounded. A confounding variable is an extraneous/lurking/nuisance variable whose influence has not been either held constant or randomized. Now two of the experimental designs listed on page 29 control confounding by making a confounding variable into an independent variable so that it can be systematically varied.*

If this is your second of the two thorough readings recommended in the Preface, then you should now be literate enough in statistics to make sense of it and be able to understand better the statistical aspects of information you encounter. As indicated at the beginning of the chapter, a very good place to go to learn more about statistics is Triola's textbook. One advantage a statistically literate person has over a person that is not is an ability to communicate with experts on statistics: statisticians and researchers. This ability is indispensable to the person who must contact on his employer's behalf a statistician, either for advice or to be a consultant. Readers wishing to find statisticians specializing in certain kinds of statistical techniques (e.g., regression analysis, analysis of variance, Bayesian statistics, process control charts, time series analysis, statistical techniques appropriate with stratified or cluster samples, and sequential analysis) might log onto the American Statistical Association's website.

---

* The bimodal and multimodal frequency distributions alluded to on page 44 exemplify confounding. Despite their names implying these distributions have two modes or more than two modes respectively, the names are actually applied to any distribution with a mode (i.e., category having the largest frequency) and one or more categories that are a few categories away from the mode whose fairly large frequencies show up as one or more additional humps, or peaks, in the graph of a frequency distribution. Bimodal and multimodal distributions are commonly interpreted as being frequencies compiled from data that describe two or more populations, rather than - as should be the case - one population. What is confounded/obscured/hidden/masked in such distributions are the frequencies of the categories that two or more populations share, which are those categories lying in between the humps.

REFERENCES

Blalock, Hubert M. Jr. <u>Social Statistics</u>. New York: McGraw-Hill, 1979 (revised second edition).

Bowley, Arthur L. <u>Elements of Statistics</u>. New York: Charles Scribner's Sons, 1907 (third edition).

Bradley, James V. <u>Distribution-Free Statistical Tests</u>. Englewood Cliffs (N.J.): Prentice-Hall, 1968.

Campbell, John L. <u>Introduction to Science and the Scientific Method</u>. Greenville(N.C): Kravits & Sons, 2025

Glass, Gene V. and Hopkins, Kenneth D. <u>Statistical Methods in Education and Psychology</u>. Boston: Allyn & Bacon, 1996 (third edition).

Guilford, J.P. <u>Psychometric Methods</u>. New York: McGraw- Hill Book Company, 1936 (first edition).

Hays, William L. <u>Statistics</u>. New York: Holt, Rinehart & Winston, 1994 (fifth edition).

Mansfield, Edwin <u>Statistics for Business and Economics</u>. New York: W.W. Norton & Company, 1983 (second edition).

Meitzen, August <u>History, Theory. And Technique of Statistics</u>. Philadelphia: American Academy Of Political And Social Science, 1891 (translation into English by Roland P. Falkner of original, in German, published in 1886). An interesting perspective of a statistician five years before statistics commenced becoming more mathematical.

Mendenhall, William; Ott, Lyman; and Larson, Richard F. <u>Statistics: A Tool for the Social Sciences</u>. North Scituate (Massachusetts): Duxbury Press, 1974 (first edition).

Miller, Irwin and Freund, John E. <u>Probability and Statistics for Engineers</u>. Englewood Cliffs (N.J.): Prentice-Hall, 1985 (third edition).

Moore, David S. <u>The Basic Practice of Statistics</u>. New York: W.H. Freeman and Company, 2000 (second edition).

Neter, John; Kutner, Michael H.; Nachtsheim, Christopher J.; and Wasserman, William <u>Applied Linear Statistical Models</u>. New York: WCB/McGraw-Hill, 1996 (fourth edition).

Porter, Theodore M. <u>The Rise Of Statistical Thinking 1820-1900</u>. Princeton (N.J.): Princeton University Press, 1986.

Roscoe, John T. <u>Fundamental Research Statistics for the Behavioral Sciences</u>. New York: Holt, Rinehard And Winston, 1975 (second edition).

Rudgley, Richard <u>The Lost Civilizations of the Stone Age</u>. New York: The Free Press, 1999.

Secrist, Horace <u>An Introduction to Statistical Methods</u>. New York: The Macmillan Company, 1917 (first edition).

Siegel, Sidney and Castellan, N. John Jr. <u>Nonparametric Statistics For The Behavioral Sciences.</u> New York: McGraw-Hill, 1988 (second edition).

Triola, Mario F. <u>Elementary Statistics</u>. Boston: Pearson Education (Addison-Wesley), 2006 (tenth edition). This is an excellent next step to learning more about statistics.

Waugh, Albert E. <u>Elements of Statistical Method</u>. New York: McGraw-Hill Book Company, 1943 (second edition).

www.ingramcontent.com/pod-product-compliance
Lightning Source LLC
Chambersburg PA
CBHW081723120626
46550CB00010B/3230